CW01305855

Control Your Stress and Enjoy Your Horse

Confidence Strategies for Pleasure Riding

by Karl Greenwood D.H.P.

"You become like the people you spend most time with. Choose wisely"

Chapter 1

Influences

Learning to know horses, read them, handle them, ride and control them is quite difficult, non-linear and not always logical. It takes years of patience and persistence, but then, that's part of the fun. During our journey, by definition, the learning experience will be filled with…, well, experiences. Experiences from which we learn. And some of those experiences will be uplifting, some scary, some will bruise and some will make us laugh out loud for joy.

If I was to ask you what makes your friends *be* your friends, chances are you'd reply with examples of the similarities in your personalities, values and shared world outlook. As social beings, we find rapport and closeness with people who we identify as like ourselves. We are fond of people who we are similar to, those who we share values with. It's with these people that we share our anxieties and worries, and in turn, we support them when things go awry. It's a thing called friendship, we can laugh at ourselves and each other, and it's a wonderful thing. At our yards and with our horses, we find mutual support in our mutual successes and problems.

The problem is, at our yards, and with our horses, (as at school), our friends are our friends. And our friends are not necessarily the best teachers. If I cast my mind back past more years than I care to admit to my school days, I had my friends on the one hand, and my teachers on the other. And never the twain would meet. I know that my school education would have been most unsatisfactory if myself and Wal (my best friend) had decided to just see what we could find to fill our lives and minds with - wander around the school and go with whatever we encountered. (But I must give credit here where it's due - Wal did teach me how to do maths, just so we could finish quicker and play graph-paper golf for the rest of the lesson. Sorry Mrs. Williams.) So just as our teachers are not our friends, our friends are not our teachers – and we might not necessarily always learn what we need to learn from them.

So as our friends are not necessarily our teachers, we employ instructors instead to teach us the lessons of riding horses. Our teachers will teach us practically the correct methods to employ, how to correct the wrong experiences and how to build on the right experiences. There are many good and valuable instructors out there with great people skills and confidence giving strategies – who may be employed by a client for one or two hours a week. For the remaining 166 hours of the week, we must rely on our memory, our own inner voices, or the insights from our friends and acquaintances.

Our friends will share our experiences emotionally, and so far, so good. We can have fun, have joy, laugh and generally enjoy convivial company.

But what about when it comes to the emotion of confidence? Or the emotion of fear? It's all very well for an experienced and accomplished instructor to say the practicalities of an exercise - "Sit Up! Push him forwards!" – but what if you just, well, just can't? Because your brain freezes up? Or maybe you can follow the instruction – but your body reacts quite differently when your instructor isn't there and you're out on a hack on your own?

My question in response would be, who do you surround yourself with when it comes to learning how to be confident? How to be practical about an emotion? Not learning how to ride as such – legs like so and hands like so - but studying how to be secure in the knowledge that you can apply that learning effectively when you need to? In fact, how to operate our brains as usefully as we operate our hands and legs.

The people we ride out with are those who share our values most – our fears and successes. They may be the most wonderful people in the world, but think about them for a minute. Are they really the best source of information on confidence? Are they confident themselves? Do they communicate their strategies for confidence successfully? I would suggest that if they do communicate their strategies for confidence successfully, then you wouldn't be reading this book.

How about their fears? Do they communicate *those* effectively? Perhaps backed up with stories and anecdotes?

And if they do communicate their fears, undoubtedly there will be resonance with our *own* fears – which are then reinforced AND backed up by a second, and much valued, opinion.

I'll try to choose my words carefully here – it would never do to be perceived as having a go at your friends! And I'm not, of course.

However, chances are, your fellow riders are not your tutors in confidence. It's even possible that those you surround yourself with, with the best of intentions, actually *erode* the confidence of those around them – even as they try to boost it. When we look for support in our darkest moments friends will naturally empathise, usually in order to allow you to be kind to yourself, with such supportive phrases as, "Well, it is scary, isn't it?" or "It's OK to be scared" or "Well, we have to remember that horse riding is the most dangerous sport you can do."

Is this ringing true?

Scary Subject (ive)

If an activity is scary or not is purely subjective. It's an opinion.

It may be scary to you, or to your friend, but not to this person or that person. However, saying "Well, it is scary, isn't it?" is a reaffirming statement that the activity IS scary, full stop. As a fact – this is scary.

In that statement, there is no room for error. It. Is. Scary. And furthermore, it confirms that your friend finds it scary too. A far weaker, but more truthful version would be "Well, *you* find that scary in your opinion". In this version, it all sounds a little alien and heartless, and is not really something you would expect a supportive friend to say – I'm sure they wouldn't be your friend for very long! There is no empathy and it is almost pointless to say, and would be of little comfort.

But it's the truth, is it not? *You* find that scary, whilst another may not. Equally, in other areas of your life, you are confident in areas that others may fear. For an easy example, we all have friends who are too scared to even go into a stable, despite our protestations that he wouldn't ever kick or bite and gives the most wonderful affection. We can clearly see that there is no danger in the situation, and that to say going into our lovely horse's stable is scary, well, it's just not.

What this realisation is pulling us round to acknowledge is that danger may be real, but fear is not. It IS dangerous to stand on a cliff edge, and no-one would argue with that. Whether the culprit of such personal risk was scared or not, the activity IS dangerous. If I stood on a cliff edge, my opinion would be that that is scary, whilst an extreme sports enthusiast standing next to me would not find it scary at all. In a climbing harness however, there is no danger....... But I'd still be scared. Standing on a cliff edge in a harness may possibly induce a great deal of fear, depending on the person, even though they know they cannot fall.

The question that has real world value is not "Is it Scary?", but instead, "Is it Dangerous?"

Danger is real. Fear is not.

To assess the danger level of something is an intellectual exercise. It is associated with words like "caution", "assessment" and "prevention" and phrases such as "taking precautions" and "risk aversion",.

None of these words or phrases have a particular emotional association with them. The recognition and assessment of danger is an intellectual exercise taking place in the intellectual and logical parts of our brain.

In contrast, fear is an emotion and takes place, unsurprisingly, in the primitive parts of our brain. The associated words and phrases are loaded with emotion – "horrifying", "terrifying", "scared", "paralysed with fear". Think about how we represent these concepts to ourselves – have you ever been rooted to the spot with danger? No. But rooted to the spot with fear? Oh yes, of course.

Our emotions are not best placed to assess danger, and yet we justify our feelings of fear by linking them to the levels of danger – when in reality they are completely separate in all but the most extreme of circumstances. When the lion bounds through the living room door, then we can allow fear and danger to be regarded as the same thing, however, in most circumstances we encounter in our civilised and ordered society, fear or danger are in effect separate processes.

The question is not whether or not an activity is scary – but whether the level of danger intrinsic to that activity is acceptable.

Is what we are doing actually dangerous?

Justifying your Fears

Which brings us to the second sentence offered by our friend to justify their fear - "Well, we have to remember that horse riding is the most dangerous sport you can do."

How often do you hear this statement, uttered as an irrefutable fact. The vast majority of riders I speak with have heard this sentiment in one form or another: the most dangerous sport, activity or hobby that one can do.

The unreal fear of riding has now been linked by our associates to the no nonsense factual reality of danger. Does this sound familiar?

Of course horse riding is in the list of the most dangerous sports. In fact, horse riding is at the top – *depending on which list you search Google for*.

However, in some listed top tens of dangerous activities, horse riding doesn't even feature. In some, it's disappointingly low down the list, behind cycling and swimming. In others, it's very close to the top. Keep searching and you'll find a top ten where horse riding is the number one.

You'll also find the number one cause of household accidents is slippers, the number one animal killer is the sheep (Apparently, they knock into the back of farmers knees and the poor farmer then hits his head on the floor. Apparently.) ………..and the number one issue with immigration is benefit fraud, or maybe the number one issue with immigration is the number of hospital staff and care workers.

Who knows. But then, even in a list where horse riding is the number one dangerous activity - what would you class horse riding? An activity? A sport? Are we looking at top level eventing? Showjumping? Rodeo? Jousting? or Happy Hackers? Or horse logging? And what exactly do we mean by dangerous? The number of fatalities? Or reported accidents? How about unreported accidents? How about anecdotal accidents? Or our friend's tales of Almost Accidents, weaving a narrative of bravery and amusement to fill a lull in the tall tales told over half a shandy?

The fact is, keep searching enough, or wait long enough, and you will find a study to back up your pre-suppositions and beliefs.

If one believes horses are dangerous in the first place, that's good enough. The "facts" will be out there for you to find.

Soon enough there will be a study to show that five pieces of fruit are NOT good for you. It will be ten, or none. Soon enough there will be a study to show that drinking eight glasses of water is not good, that tea is hydrating or fluoride in water is bad for the teeth.

Wait long enough, and you will find a study to back up your pre-suppositions and beliefs – we all remember the study that said red wine in good for the health, don't we?

But we must entertain the slim possibility, the concept which must not be uttered, the quiet thought which is being swamped in the well-meaning cacophony of tales of fear-smelling broncos, stories of behaviour-altering brain tumours and cautions of hospital filling chestnut mares – we must entertain the possibility that possibly, just possibly, horses are safe.

It's a possibility that whispers, and never shouts. But it whispers with an irrefutable confidence in its own existence. If we can quiet the noise of those who surround us – and I include Facebook posts, social media awareness campaigns, news reports and 24 hours in A&E – we can take note of the possibility that horses are safe.

Horses are safe.

Even perhaps, even more than that - horses are fun!

Yes, Fun! Remember that?

We must remember what brought us to horse riding in the first place. The mental image of how we would like to be that first brought us to the saddle. A mental image, probably formed in our childhood years, of beaches and wind and hair….

None of us are forced to ride horses. Very few leisure riders are forced to ride. We do it for the pleasure, the fun and the enjoyment. How often do we allow ourselves to remember that this is the purpose of horse riding? If you don't like horse riding, there are plenty of other hobbies out there. Tennis, swimming, cycling, watercolours and the tuba are all there for us. No one has to ride horses unless they want to.

Too many riders return from a ride with the only emotion is being filled with relief that they are still alive. And that's no fun at all, in fact, the very opposite of fun. Yet here we are, spending *huge* amounts of money and time. We forget to acknowledge to ourselves that we are doing this because it's fun, because we love it, because it makes us feel good. But honestly – when did you last say that about your horses and riding? That simple acknowledgement can turn around our outlook and make the whole experience of riding vibrant and enjoyable again. If you can genuinely look inside yourself and find no fun or pleasure in riding horses, then stop. If there is joy, however, then why not focus on it? You always get more of what you focus on, so it'll be nice to get more pleasure.

In conversation - that I either have myself, hear from my clients, or observe riders having between themselves, - either on social media, in the pages of magazines or riders just chatting generally: the perception of the dangers of horse riding is at odds with my own experiences in my professional day to day career.

Forgive me, I get so passionate about my subject matter, that I completely forgot to introduce myself. My name is Karl Greenwood, and I am a Hypnotherapist and stunt rider. We also teach the sports of Horseback Archery and Dzhigitovka (a Russian sport of sword, lance, pistol, knife throwing, archery and gymnastics all off the back of a horse), and take Trick Riding, Dzhigitovka and Jousting Shows out to entertain at County Shows, Castles and Royal Shows.

It all sounds very exciting and jolly brave, and the action photos, articles and pictures that adorn our walls bear testament to our experiences from the so-called extremes of horse riding.

As a consequence of our experiences, I, along with my wife Zana, were able to create a one-off Rider Confidence course currently running in Hemel Hempstead in Hertfordshire – a unique combination of Hypnotherapy and practical exercises on trained stunt horses to show everyday riders how to cope with rears, spins and falls. The course is a great success and has helped many riders regain their perspective on riding and return to enjoying their horses.

I digress. As I was saying, before I rudely interrupted myself, the general public perception of the dangers of horse riding is at odds with my own experiences in my professional day to day career. Very at odds. In fact, almost the very opposite. The dangers of horse riding - even in the extremes - is simply not anything like at the level that is perpetuated and propagated as fact across the leisure horse community.

And it's not just me and my industry – wherever people work professionally with horses the opinion is that horses are *not* intrinsically dangerous.

However, the first thing I need to get across to clients, on-line forums and communities of other riders is that we are NOT brave. We ARE, however, experienced risk assessors. We have contingency plans, we are trained for a job and we keep ourselves trained for that job, and from our career perspective we can help you with your horse riding.... but .... we're not brave. It's just that riding horses in conditions that some may view as extreme is our day to day life. I don't know what you do for a living but I do know that if I were to come into your work, I would be feeling just as nervous as the people who come into my stables - especially if your jobs have actual real world consequences such as working in finance or education or in hospital. Very (subjectively) scary stuff. But hopefully under your guidance and with your friendship at the end of the day I will be happily working away with you, feeling confident and putting all the right components in the right place.

The second thing that we have to get - into both our conscious AND our subconscious minds – as suggested earlier - is that horses are NOT intrinsically dangerous. In fact, I will go further…..

Horses are Safe

Fundamentally, horses are safe. They are! That is why we ride them! And why we've ridden them for thousands of years. And, that is why we don't ride, say, lions. Don't come on my lion riding confidence course!! My lion riding confidence course does really really badly, for a very good reason.

10,000 years ago when one villager said I'm going to try to ride Dobbin to work and the other villager said I'm going to try to ride Leo to work, well. Only one of them came back. That's when we realised.

Horses. Are. Safe.

Lions Are Not Safe. But Horses Are Safe. That's why we ride them, and we don't ride lions. We ride horses for a reason. Us, and millions of other people over countless centuries.

Now I know there will be a queue of riders with their own stories of disaster ready to refute my claim that horses are safe. However, horses are safe in the same way that Volvo's are safe, or air travel is safe. We have all seen stories of aeroplane disasters on the news, and Volvo could not put out an advert which specifically said "Volvo's are safe", because someone somewhere would pop up with a story of their Uncle Jeff who walks with a permanent limp now……. but the common knowledge is that Volvo's and air travel are safe. Horses are also safe.

What we are saying, in all three cases, is that in the vast vast vast vast vast vast and vast majority of journeys, Volvos and aeroplanes are safe. As are horses.

Not only are horses safe, but they're getting safer.

Us leisure riders don't really need horses to get to work and back again. We've basically only got the leisure & sport industry left, and so the leisure horses are the bloodlines that the breeders are interested in. It's simply supply and demand that means on the whole the good leisure horses are the lines that will be bred from. The screaming stallion that killed everybody but was really good pulling a coal barge for a week and a half of nothing but a bucket of grain isn't really of any use anymore, so his bloodlines have faded out through not having a market. (Please, draught horse enthusiasts, before you start writing - I know)

I digress. It is a fact that supply and demand means that inevitably horses are being bred safer and safer for the leisure market in this country.

Not only are the horses being bred safer – to fulfil the supply and demand chain - but the equipment we use with our equines is getting safer too. We have safety stirrups, non-slip numnahs, ergonomic girths, better designed, fitted and manufactured bits, hi-viz jackets, … the list goes on and on. The future holds evermore increasing technological advances to make things even safer. Air jackets, 3D scanning saddle trees, carbon fibre motion absorbing technologies, the list goes on in ever improving ways. All of this is making horses safer.

Furthermore, we have ever improving comprehensive research into animal comfort and psychology, training programs and training systems. We understand animal psychology better, and we have greater resources of information in Google and eBooks and in references than we have ever had before.

Even on a personal level, our general knowledge as riders is so much more than it used to be. If a horse is misbehaving now, anybody you ask will automatically say," Check it's saddle, check it's tack, check it's teeth". Because we are SO much better informed. That never happened when I was a kid!

And even when things do go wrong, we are so much better protected, and prepared, then we ever have been before. Back protectors, air jackets, safety hats, kite mark standards, stirrup leathers that come off the saddle and safety stirrups all go to averting risk.

As well as acknowledging that horses are safe, (and getting safer!), and our personal protection is making riding safer, we mustn't lose sight of the fact that, even when it does go wrong, *we are usually fine anyway*! Most of the world doesn't have the nice lifestyle we have - with the luxury of cars and roads and electricity - but instead rely 100% on their equines - horses, mules and donkeys - to carry on their lives and work, So as we have sat reading this text for the last half an hour, how many of those millions of people, currently interacting with their equines, have suffered some sort of negative interaction today? A small proportion of a large number of horsepeople is still, however, a significant number of people.

In the last half hour – hundreds if not thousands of people have for certain fallen off, been trodden on, kicked, barged through, squashed against the wall, dropped their packs, turned the cart over, slipped on a rock, whatever. These things happen, and they've happened to people today, right now, with no safety hats or jackets or special training or anything whatsoever.

And did these people die?

No, they have just got back on their horses and carried on their day, with hardly an after-dinner anecdote to tell the family. This tiny percentage of horsepeople is still in the hundreds, if not thousands – of the millions working with their equines at this very moment. Many people every day have mishaps with horses and there's nothing to report. Because, even when it goes wrong, it is usually fine. If it wasn't fine, if tens of thousands of people died or were injured by their equines every day, don't you think we'd know? But it doesn't, because they don't. They don't because horses are safe.

And that's just in the last half hour. We've been riding horses for thousands of years! How many millions and billions of journeys have completed without incident from those millions of people over millions of days? And, as already mentioned, even when it went wrong, it was usually fine. Possibly in a Jane Austen novel, the returning avenger galloped over the rain-swept moor on a stormy night, the clanging of the storm bells of his abandoned ship being carried mournfully by the howling wind like pall-bearers of doom, his horse put its foot in a hole and the antagonist was flung from his horse – killing him instantly – ……..but that is called a *plot device*. It is not a documentary! A plot device is everything to do with arranging for the hero and heroine to find their destinies, clasping hands to bosoms and breathlessly declaring undying passion – and it is *nothing* to do with the factual day to day life of millions of horse riders taking millions of journeys, the vast majority without incident, and the vast majority of those remaining journeys *with* incidents being absolutely fine.

We even have our own life experiences to fall back on in this regard. How many rides have you been on in your life? A hundred? More? And of each hundred rides, how many resulted in an injury? Not a bruise, or a shock, but an actual injury? One per hundred? One percent? Less than one per hundred? Less than one percent? That's an over 99% success rate. How about if we only include injuries that sent you to hospital? Most falls, as mentioned above, turn out fine anyway. So, only counting falls that sent you to hospital, what's your success rate? For some, that's a 100% success rate – and yet they would still describe themselves as likely to fall or get hurt. 99%-100% successful rider, versus 0% -1% victim.

It only took 52% for us to stop being European!

So firstly, horses are safe, and getting safer - and secondly, even when it goes wrong it's fine for the vast, vast, vast majority of the time.

When lion riding goes wrong, that's different. My lion riding course sells really, really badly.

You are more capable that you realise.

So, you don't need to be brave, and horses are safe. And they're getting safer. And even when it goes wrong it's fine in the overwhelmingly vast majority of the time, even if we don't take any action. The next thing that we need to introduce to our subconscious mind, is that, when it goes wrong and we DO have to take action, when we have to do something to stop a situation turning into a mess - *we already have the ability to cope.*

Out on our horses, when the time comes to take action to minimise our risk, riders tend to freeze rather than act.

Why is that, do you think? Why would we freeze rather than take action?

One possible reason is that, in our sheltered lives, we so rarely find ourselves in a life-or-death situation, that when we do find ourselves on our horses with the potentially fatal consequences if we mess it up, we're overwhelmed and unable to act. We seize up.

How does that sound? I'd say it sounds plausible, but then I'd go on to say, "What nonsense."

We cope with life and death situations ALL the time, EVERY DAY, perfectly easily, perfectly capably.

Let me give an example.

Take swimming.

We all know how potentially dangerous water can be, especially if it's unfamiliar waters in unfamiliar place. And yet, even though we're aware of the danger, and we are aware of the terrible trouble we *could* find ourselves in, none the less, we will happily spend *thousands* of pounds, and travel *thousands* of miles to unfamiliar seas, where the water is warm, so we can spend *even longer* bathing in it! Of course, we take sensible precautions, to make sure that we can cope with this life and death situation. We will ask at the hotel where the safe place to swim is, we will be aware of signs on the beach, and swim between the flags or where there's a lifeguard or whatever.

And if this example doesn't resonate with you, if you don't swim, there is no shortage of life and death situations which you cope with all the time to choose from instead. Riding a bicycle, crossing the road, driving a car, walking down the stairs in a pair of novelty slippers, any of these situations could end in disaster, but don't. Why not? Because you take the correct precautions to make sure you're safe. And, furthermore, you think nothing of it.

    Let's take driving as an example. If you don't drive then think of riding a bicycle, crossing the street, whatever. The mental process is the same.

    Ok. So you're driving down the motorway. You come to your junction, and it's one of those big junctions with a huge slip road, going up to a major roundabout. Six possible lanes of traffic, and you have to drive onto the roundabout and continue your journey.

    Automatically, you take sensible precautions to make sure you bring this experience into your ability to ensure success. You feel your level of arousal raise, maybe a feeling of adrenaline will begin, as you realise it is time to take decisive action. You adapt your surroundings to increase the chances of success - maybe turn down the radio, or call over your shoulder... "Shut up, kids! I've got to concentrate!" You do whatever it is to match your actions to your state of arousal to cope with the situation you find yourself in

    And you *do* cope - easily- with the life and death situation that you are now coming into.

    Your state of arousal is up. You start to assess the multitude of factors that you now have to deal with. You take notice of potential dangers. Notice, for example, any large lorries on one side or the other of you, (or both!). You have to be aware of the road signs so that you get in the correct lane, and all the other signs advising road conditions, and at the same time become aware that the traffic lights are on green. (.... And traffic lights on green is the worst one, because you can never judge if they will have changed to red by the time you get up to them!) You check in your rear view mirror, that the car behind you isn't too close in case the lights do change to red and you have to stop, read the paint on the road, change your gears, swap your lane etc. etc.

You find the gap in the traffic, and change your lane, and anticipate where your opportunity to pull onto the roundabout is. Even though you are heading into a potentially dangerous situation, you have every faith in your ability to negotiate that situation, and carry on your journey to work, or to see your mum, whatever or whatever.

And you use these abilities irrelevant of the fact that you can feel the adrenaline increase in your body as you enter a potentially dangerous situation.

What you *don't* do, is think, "It'll be alright, …. positive thinking, Kids! I've read a book on the Law of Attraction … the Universe will look after us!", put a paper bag over your head, and press the pedal to the floor, trusting in the Universe and a Positive Mindset to glide you across the junction in a Cloud Of Confidence. It doesn't work like that. Your confidence is in *you*, not the universe or the situation. Your confidence is in you, and is not swayed by the presence or absence of adrenaline.

You have absolute confidence in negotiating this junction, just as you did with the last junction, and just as you will do with the next 10 or 20 junctions. You are 100% confident in your abilities. Interestingly, this is still the case even if you refer to yourself as an unconfident driver.

And it's the same for riding a bicycle and crossing the road, and innumerable other situations. If you mess it up, you could make a real mess.

So you don't.

Therefore, it follows that if you can cope in that life and death situation, or this life and death situation, (and you can, and you have, and you do. On a regular basis.), then what is the difference with coping when in a situation with your horse?

"A-ha!" My clients say at this point. "The difference is that my horse *has a mind of it's own.*"

Well - as you may expect by now - please allow me to retort.

When you get into a car as a passenger, and you ask the driver if it would be necessary to put on your seatbelt, it is very seldom that the driver will turn to you and say, "Oh yes! Buckle up! I tell you now, I am a really s*** driver."

Very seldom do they say that. Usually, what they say is something like, "Yes. You put your seatbelt on - it's not *me*, it's just that you don't know what nutters are out there."

Exactly.

Let's just take a moment to think about exactly what that statement implies here.

So what we are saying, is that we are perfectly happy to contemplate the thought that out on the road there may be up to four million drivers, any one of which could be a complete nutter, each in charge of half a ton of metal and explosive liquids travelling at speeds up to one hundred miles per hour.

We agree that we are quite prepared to cope with that, but when we are presented with our horse, who has a brain the size of a broad bean and will do the same predictably unpredictable things day in and day out, suddenly we say, "But it has a mind of it's own!" and we can't cope!

What nonsense. We clearly CAN cope, it's just that we have to *make the decision* to cope. Like we do when we drive in amongst other drivers.

Please allow me to continue the driving analogy a little further, won't be long I promise. We will make our way back to horses soon.

On your way around your daily life, I suspect that you travel quite a lot in a car. To work, to the shops, you know, normal stuff. And on your way to your destination, of course, you engaged in a series of spectacular, brave, and amazing stunts during your journey. Of course you did! Travelling along a single carriageway road at 60 miles an hour, lorries coming the other way at 60 miles an hour, closing speed of 120 miles an hour, and you passed so close, that if both drivers stretched out their hands, they could probably high five each other as they went past.

Wow! Amazing!

Of course, the reality is that you drive past traffic at 60 miles an hour all the time - and think nothing of it.

If we were to change the frame of reference, you can fully appreciate your acts of skill and derring-do. I certainly do. Let's have a closer look at what you do so capably. Let's just reframe this particular stunt, by taking this particular piece of action to the vast deserts in America, where they attempt land speed records on long, smooth, vast, flat, dried lake beds.

OK, here we are. It's hot and dry, and that hard-baked ground is as flat as a mill pond in all directions. Heat haze rises to make mirages of water, and probably a lizard will skitter somewhere - because lizards like a cliché as much as the next reptile.

You get the idea.

In this dead flat dead landscape we will put the lorry up there on the horizon, shimmering through the distorted rising thermals. You can get into this lovely Ford Ka down here, the radio looping to a slow and mournful mid-west slide guitar riff.

On the word "Action", you accelerate rapidly up to 60 miles an hour towards the lorry across this vast dried up ancient lake bed. The lorry is accelerating up to 60 miles an hour towards you, thick clouds of dust spiralling away behind the ever accelerating juggernaught as it speeds towards you. Closing speed of 120 miles an hour. In the middle of this vast lake bed, you are to drive past each other SO close, that if you leant out, you could high five the driver.

Wheeeeeeeeeeeee – ummmmmmmmm!!!

Wow.

Given this new frame of reference, you would undoubtedly demand stunt wages for this particular piece of action.

Let's up the ante even more!

Now, there's no Ford Ka. There's just you – standing, in the desert, twiddling your thumbs and sweating in the heat. Lizards skitter over your worn cowboy boots. If you squint against the glare of the sun and through the haze, you can just see on the shimmering horizon the mechanics changing the engine of the lorry for an enhanced racing engine, one which will now go at 120 miles an hour towards you. In climbs the driver, and for the first few seconds you find it difficult to fathom the exact moment of the lorry starting to head towards you, until the haze of dust thickens and begins to rotate behind the cab. You now see signs of movement as the lorry seems to creep imperceptibly closer, clouds of thick spiralling dust obscuring the horizon like an avenging demon. Suddenly your perception realises the speed of the thing, this huge lorry careering towards you, 60, 70, 80, eerily silent, 90, closer and closer, the roar of the engine suddenly arising like a storm of sound, 100, 120, bearing down on you where you stand.

And…

And….

AND……

And "*WHOOOOOOSSSSHHHHHH!* "

Zooming past you at 120 miles an hour, so close that you could lean over and high five the driver.

Well, you would certainly want stunt wages for that, don't you think?

And yet, you do the same thing, all the time, every day, without thinking anything of it.

If we can reframe one simple, safe, everyday action to appear more dangerous than it is, then we can go the other way, and reframe something we are perceiving as dangerous, back down to the simple, safe, every day action that it is.

It's a fact that when I ask, most of my clients will say that they used to be more confident than they are today. However, the *actions* they are doing today - jumping, trotting, cantering or whatever - are *exactly* the same actions that they did when they were confident! Therefore, somehow, between then and now, somewhere along the line they have reframed those actions from being everyday actions into being something more dangerous than it truly is.

So, if you can reframe in one direction, then you can reframe in the other direction too. Just as my persuasive words showed you how you could perceive something to be either everyday or dangerous, so *somebody's* persuasive words have persuaded you that the safe and everyday actions of horse riding is somehow more dangerous than it is.

Who's been doing that? Reframing your hobby for you? The thing you love to do?

I'm sorry to say, it's the people who have your best interests at heart. It's the people you surround yourself with, the friends who want to share their nervousness with you, the feeders and relishers of your - and their - limitations and anxiety. It's also the posts you read on Facebook, social media, internet journalism and the stories of disaster, and the gossip, speculation, dramatization and sometimes pure fiction that surrounds the equine environment.

"You were lucky"

We have already considered the thousands of people who have fallen off even while we read this book, and just get up again and get on with their day. The normal outcome of falling from your horse, is that you get up and get on with your day. That's the usual outcome.

But, Facebook groups, awareness campaigns and horse magazines trying to shift a few journals, or even well meaning friends trying to be supportive, will "supportively" chastise us in a very serious voice,

"Oooooh! That could've been nasty. *You* were lucky. "

No, you were not lucky. You were normal. Riders get on, riders fall off, riders get on again, and riders fall off again. And that's what happens.

And as the thousands of people all around the world currently working their equines show us - it's normal to not be hurt.

Overwhelmingly normal not to be hurt.

Don't get me wrong, bad luck does happen, bad luck might happen on horses, passing lorries, in Volvo's and on aeroplanes but on the whole, in the vastly larger majority of rides, drives, flights and interactions, nothing untoward happens. When your ride on your horse heads south unexpectedly, in the vast vast vast majority of cases, the rider is unhurt and all that happens is that the rider gets back on.

You can imagine that, in our work at the Centre of Horseback Combat, and in filming, and in jousting shows and trick riding shows, we fall off. A lot. Yes, it happens. Sometimes on purpose, and with a wage for it, but of course, sometimes accidentally too.

If someone was to come in the door of The Centre of Horseback Combat now, and announce to the room, "Zana's fallen off!", how do you think the room would react?

Well, first things first, we would, obviously, enquire as to the outcome of that fall. "Oh! Is she alright?"

"Yes."

A confused silence would follow. Because that's the reaction it deserves.

"Um, well, can you go and get on with it please? I'm trying to write a book?"

Compare that reaction to the reaction from your typical livery yard. The door bursts open, our excited informant comes flying into the room, and declares loudly "Oh my god! Sam's fallen off!"

ALL the coffee goes up in the air! *Everybody* rushes out.

"Sam! Sam! Are you alright?"

Sam's coming down the path, leading Rocky, tears cascading "I'm OK, I'm OK… I'm just a bit shocked. "

And there'll be clucking and fussing and drama and what-iffing and everything else.

And you can be sure somebody will be running around saying, "Ooooooh! *You* were lucky!"

No, you weren't lucky. You were normal. It's normal not to be hurt. There's normal, and there's unlucky.

Beware who you surround yourself with.

And don't forget to include those Facebook posts from horse magazines – the articles that seem to be absolutely dedicated to making us terrified of horse riding!

These cheap rag spin offs trawl the world, through millions of uneventful horse rides around the globe, to find those bad luck tales and put them right in front of us in our living rooms, every day. These stories will do the rounds, get picked up over and over again. Quite often you will find a horror story doing the rounds, and it takes someone in the comments to point out "Hang on, this was six years ago."

Horse magazines' Facebook posts are literally trawling all of time and space to make out horses are dangerous. Magazines, road awareness groups, individuals wanting to seem exciting.

Invite these posts into your life with extreme caution!!!

They are not there to help you.

Para-Olympian in Horror Fall!

There was one particular Facebook post from last year. It sticks in my mind because it was so typical of the nonsense that gets bandied about. You may have seen it. The title was, Para Olympian in Horror Fall. Not just horror, but Horror. In capitals. Horror.

Reading further, it transpires that a Para Olympian, in Rio, with cerebral palsy, had been in the arena when her horse had spooked, and had fallen from her horse. The officials in the arena immediately ran to her aid, and as a precaution concealed any potential drama with a screen. She was duly taken to hospital.

In her own words the staff at the arena, and the staff at the hospital were simply great. She was treated quickly, efficiently and well, and, when all was said and done, her injury was a bruised ankle.

Now, I don't know about you, but if I had cerebral palsy, and I had fallen from a spooky horse, and ended up with a bruised ankle, well, I would consider that a *dream* fall. Just the kind of fall you hope for, (except for the bruising.)

But the title ran – Para-Olympian in Horror Fall!

Sensationalism.

Here is another thing. Sometimes it is irrelevant if the original post is sensible or not – because the comments posted underneath from all the world and sundry whip themselves up into an absolute frenzy! One particular post was from a friend of mine, who had a rotational fall at a cross country fence, and the horse had rolled onto and over her leg. The rider very capably jumped up and jumped on, set off and completed the course.

About a year later, Facebook put up one of those Share a Memory from a year ago posts. Perhaps a different mood had settled upon her, but for some reason, this particular girl, who should have known better, put up the video with the caption, "I can't believe I walked away."

The comments below went into meltdown! "Oh my god!"" You were lucky!"" That happened to my mum! Thank god she had her riding hat and back protector on! The horse rolled right over her legs!" Pages and pages of exclamations and drama, pictures of disaster and tales of trauma!

(I've always wondered how exactly does a hat and back protector help her mum's legs?)

Expressing our own fears in tenuous links to irrelevant articles in such a public place as social media really won't help anyone ride more safely. It just sends our anxieties up. People like to grab drama and play the "What if" game. People spread and exaggerate tales to paint themselves as the hero, the bravest, the luckiest, the unluckiest or the most daring. But ultimately it is to our detriment if we take *any* value to them other that a vacuous comment offered for no reason other than to offer a reaction.

My friend wasn't lucky, she was normal. And so was her friend's mum. The normal outcome of falling off, rearing, falling over......is that you're fine. Why not do as I do, and amuse yourself by reading into these posts and articles when they occur, reading past the emotion and distilling out the facts. you'll see these ludicrous posts and comments everywhere, simply everywhere - including in the conversations you have with other riders.

The vast vast vast outcome of riding horses is that you just get to where you're going – and even in the very small percentage that something goes wrong, overwhelmingly, you're fine.

But please don't apply that to riding lions.

Chapter 2

Capabilities

So we can, and we do, regularly cope with life and death situations. Every day, all the time. You'll be glad to hear I'm going to stop using the example of a slip road from the motorway onto a busy junction and get back to horses now, rather than cars, but we'll be bringing some of the lessons, skills, coping mechanisms and life experiences with us and transferring them from the one area of our life to another.

If you would be so kind as to allow me, I would like to take you on a little journey now, to share with you some of the work that we do in our day-to-day life in filming. It is my equine equivalent of driving a busy junction - the cascade of stimuli which bombard us when we leave the motorway and go on to those large roundabouts. During my work on horses, I get in some hectic situations, but no more hectic than negotiating the many complex hazards in life.

During filming, there is some woods, just outside Farnham as it happens, part owned by a famous Hollywood director, which consists of four wooded hillsides all coming down together to meet in a central clear-cut valley.

This is where all the battle scenes get filmed, on these four hillsides. Each hillside has a different characteristic.

The first hillside is, simply, a wooded hillside.

The second hillside has the trees permanently connected to gas jets, so that with a flick of a switch, the movie makers can turn the forest into a fiery inferno. (You know it, of course – we all saw Gladiator. The first scene where the Romans were fighting the Germanic tribes, running down the hill all on fire with the beautiful wolf running alongside, remember?)

It's amazing to watch the trees get turned on and off throughout the day. You hear the order come over the radio, "Light Up!", and Whoosh!, the trees are all on fire. Then they shout, "Cuuuut!" And, - Whoomph! - All the fire disappears. It's just the most incredible thing.

You have all seen these wooded hillsides. Gladiator ambushed the Germanic tribes through the fire, Robin Hood's castle was CGI'd on top of this hillside here. The third hillside is almost bare trees sticking up here and there, and the last hillside is just a few burnt stumps, just a muddy incline for War Horse to pull a First World War cannon up, the old tearjerker.

In fact, once you are familiar with these woods, you cannot watch a film without seeing them absolutely everywhere - in every production. (And there's public footpaths go through them as well, so you see the same people walking their terriers every time, wandering past 200 knights sitting in the rain going, "Can you get me a cup of coffee love, please?")

So anyway, I digress. Back to my scene setting.

There's 200 knights at the top of the hill, ready to run down through the burning trees and have a battle. So that means two hundred horses, and as you know when horses get together they get a little bit jiggy anyway.

Then the crew set fire to the trees - which doesn't really help calm the horses down at all.

You're looking down the hill, thinking, "I'll go to the left of this bush, and then the right of that stump, then out into the valley, and I can have the room to draw my sword". (By the way, just check that your horses used to swords before you get there, - it would be sad to negotiate all those obstacles and then have it leap away from a piece of bamboo! True story.)

But, as you know from your gas fires at home, gas fires do not make smoke.

So they've got the smoke machines.

Big hissing, cloud making machines, blasting smoke down long, white, convoluted tubes, snaking their way just out of shot around the hedges, which have tennis ball sized holes in the side of the tubes to allow the smoke out. Pssssssssssss! Pss-pss-pss-pss-pss-pssssssssssss!

And, as you can guess the smoke almost never goes across camera. So they have these BIG wind machines, making sure that the smoke is pushed across camera to where they want it to be. Huge fans attached to the back of tractor units.

"WhrrrrrrrrrrRRRRRRRRRRRRRRRRRRRRRRRRRR!!!!!!!!!", go the wind machines.

"PssssssssssssssssSSSSSSSSSSHHHHHHHTTTTT!!!!!!", go the smoke machines

Then they send the helicopter up just above tree level, to film the whole thing.

WhuggawhuggawhuggaWHUGGAWHUGGAWHUGGA!!!!".

The trees are swaying underneath the downdraft, the smoke machine is hissing away, the wind machine is whirling, and the trees are on fire.

The horses now are fairly jiggy, to be honest.

And then, THEN, (and this is the worst bit), then……. then they do NOTHING AT ALL for about 20 minutes! While they check the actor's hair, or he gets reminded of his lines, or has a little moment to try and find his Muse.

And as you can guess, when the horses get going it's not nearly as bad, but the anticipation!

That is the worst bit. The anticipation.

As you can imagine, it is chaos. It sort of holds together for a little bit, kind of like…… Have you ever made popcorn in a pan? That sort of holds together for a little bit, then one goes and then another goes before you know it, pop pop pop pop!

There are people falling off everywhere. But as we now have seen, the outcome of falling off is that….. well, you get back on and that's it.

That person over there has fallen off, - you alright? - yeah. Now this one's falling off! Are YOU alright? -Yep yep.

Whoah! Now it's my turn now, wahay! No no I'm alright.

Up you get.

"Hold my stirrup would you?"

Horses are spinning, jumping, lurching forward, rearing up and slipping over.

Oh, allow me to deviate from my tale. A quick word about horses rearing and slipping over. It is jolly dangerous and I am not belittling that at all.

However, we must not get sensationalist, even in this extreme situation. Whilst we would assume, that if a horse rears up and falls over backwards, we would definitely be squished, in MY

EXPERIENCE, at endless live shows and filming days, I must have seen this particular problem AT LEAST thirty times if not more.

Now, you can find me stories, of course – tales of people who have had the horse rear and fall over, and have come a cropper, maybe you know them yourself, maybe they were you, - and facebook will certainly tell me! – But, in my experience, seeing this dangerous reaction over thirty times on film sets and in live shows - the worst injury I've seen, is a broken finger.

And this is for a particularly nasty event. This just goes to show, that even in the extremes of the extreme, *you are usually fine!*

(And we were on £395 a day, so the young lady in question, was not going to let a broken finger, stop her from earning that money, see the medic and finish the day!)

I digress. Back to our hill, woods, 200 horses, bamboo swords, fire, smoke, wind machines and helicopter.

So finally they call To Action, and we are on our way.

"Chaaaaaaarge!"

How we arrange matters, by the way, is on the Monday in Tuesday, we're all in plain riding clothes, so that we haven't handicapped ourselves further with problems of costume, or flags, or armour, flaming torches or whatever. We run through the action maybe 10 times before lunch, 10 times after lunch, on the Monday and the Tuesday. Then we put the armour on for Wednesday's rehearsal, get them used to that - and Thursday and Friday it's lights camera action and we film the actual thing.

There we are.

Now, you would assume, that, if YOU were riding on the bridleways around Farnham, and you accidentally took the wrong bridleway, and you found yourselves amongst these knights, charging down the hill, through the fire, and the smoke, and the wind, and the helicopter - you would assume, that you are DEFINITELY, Going To Die.

Wouldn't you?

Definitely going to die.

However, allow me to retort! There are two hundred Knights, performing the same action, and they *don't* die!

So that's odds of two hundred knights, to one of you, that you're wrong, they're right, and you *don't* die. You just get to the bottom of the hill, turn around, and reset to the beginning of the scene, back up the hill.

And, furthermore, those two hundred riders went through that action TEN times before lunch. That's ten times for each knight, and there are two hundred knights. That's two thousand runs. *Two thousand* to one says that you don't die.

And ten times after lunch!

That makes *four thousand runs* in a day, four thousand to one that they're correct, you're mistaken, and you don't die. You just get to the bottom of the hill, turn around, and reset to the beginning back up the hill.

And that's just on Monday.

Four thousand runs in a day. There's five days in a week, that's TWENTY THOUSAND to one that you are wrong, they are right, and you don't die. You just get to the bottom of the hill, turn around, and reset to the beginning back up the hill.

And that's one scene, from one film.

Take the amount of scenes in a film, and the amount of films that have been made since the 1920's, and you're soon in the millions to one.

Millions to one says that Everything Is Fine.

Actually, Millions to None. Now that is my kind of odds.

THIS is what horses are capable of. It's worth taking on board. This is what horses are capable of.

This is what riders are capable of.

This is what YOU are capable of.

In our daily riding lives, we vastly underuse our horses' capabilities.

Think of that next time somebody says, "Well, it IS bin day."

"This doesn't apply to me."

Hold on there, though. I know what you're thinking. There is always a little part of our brains to say, "This does not apply to me."

"Doesn't apply to me."

"MUST not apply to me!"

A little part of a negative thought pattern, it comes up with all kinds of excuses, to pretend that this is not correct or in some weird way applies to everyone else, but does not apply to me. However much logic, reason, experience, expertise or explanation is applied – this does not apply to me.

Here it goes.

"Well, they've got *Special* Horses!"

Sigh

Well, yes, that's true. They do have Special Horses. But those Special Horses, you can be sure, are NOWHERE near you. Those Special Horses are at the front - they're at the front, making a protective cocoon around the actors, making sure that they're past any explosions or surprises! The Special Filming Horses are nowhere near you and the rest of the warriors.

YOUR horses were bought at market on the Saturday, and they are in the scene on the Monday.

I'll say that again, because it is worth repeating. Bought at market on the Saturday, and they are in the scene on the Monday.

Think of your horse. Your horse, the one at home, that you ride. That horse, if you were to take it to market, would be sold on the Saturday, and doing that battle scene on the Monday.

That's right.

Our negative brains have another try. "A-ha!" Cries the negative side of your brain, " …..but in that case, they will have Special *Riders*!"

That's it. Of course. Special Riders. Super talented. Super capable. Super riders.

Do you really think, that you can get *two hundred* super-capable, super-talented, super riders, all together, all available, at one time, at one place?

On a *weekday*??

That's not going to happen. Super Capable, Super Able, Super Riders will be busy running their super capable super businesses.

Charlotte Du Jardin is NOT doing this battle scene.

If you have EVER tried to get *any* sort of project together, ever, you will know just how difficult it is to get reliable and talented people to be there for you. If you have ever tried to even get a pub quiz team together, of four people with a general awareness of the world, then you will know how hard it is.

Imagine trying to get two hundred super capable riders together who are available on a weekday!

It's just not going to happen. The fact is, you get anyone you can. The drivers. The yard owners. The horse suppliers. The racing yard, the hunt, the grooms, the family. At least some of the knight will be females. (With visors down.)

The riders are just normal people. Like you, like me.

When you sit in the lunch tent, or the breakfast tent, the gossip and chat is the same gossip and chat you will get anywhere. I don't like this, I don't like that, don't go near the left side of the woods there's a dip in the ground or whatever, be aware of this bit here. Usual stuff.

One soon realises that our special riders are just normal people, like you, and me, on normal horses, who *only* advantage or speciality is that they have the added experience that it'll be fine.

The ONLY difference between YOU and THEM is……

THEY KNOW IT CAN BE DONE

They didn't always know it can be done, of course. They had to find out. Maybe some of the girls had begged to be in a film, envisioning some Victorian romance, galloping in floaty dresses across the moors and beaches to their destiny, filled with heartbreak, flushed complexions, unrequited love and the Consumption. "Sure! You can come ride in a film!" …and Boom! Make sure the visors down and look out for that dip on the left-hand side of the hillside.

The ONLY difference between you and them is that they know it can be done. (And they are a few thousand pounds better off at the end of the week.)

And at the end of the week, you can be sure that the chat goes like this….. "Oooh, yes, please, do give me a call for the next one………here's my mobile, and my landline ….. and my mum just in case………"

This is what horses are capable of.

Let me put it another way. Do you ever go to horse trials? I do! I love 'em! And what do you do when you go to horse trials? You spend your money getting into the gate, then go and get an ice cream, and then you say, "C'mon! Let's go find the water jump!"

And why do you go to the water jump?

Simple. You go to the water jump to see people get fired off.

That's it. You don't go to see wonderful horsemanship, because there is much better horsemanship at the more complex jumps elsewhere on the course. All sorts of novelty jumps and complex combinations. You go to the water jump to see people get fired off. That's it. You, and the hundreds of other spectators.

Then what? You wander round, find the bar, go and buy some expensive clothes and tack, and then, just before you go home, you say, "Let's just pop down the water jump once more."

Between us all, ……you, me, and the other thousands of spectators across the years, we must have seen hundreds, if not thousands, of people fired off at the water jump.

Once, …….*ONCE!*,……. in 2003, Zara Phillips was airlifted to hospital.

Gosh it was exciting. Big yellow helicopter came down, off she went, to the hospital, where she was declared as fine.

And which is the one we remember? The thousands of people who got fired off then got up again? Or that one time, 15 years ago, when the air ambulance came down?

You would assume, that if, one day, you were going for a lovely ride, and you accidentally took the wrong bridle path, and found yourself hurtling down the hill towards the water jump, you would think, that you are definitely, definitely, Going To Die.

However, the fact is, *there are thousands to one*, spectators and riders, who say you are wrong. Yes, you are going to fall off. Yes, you are going to get wet. And no, you're not going to die.

I'll say it again, along with the chorus of billions of horse rides over thousands of years…..Horses Are Safe. Mostly nothing goes awry, and even when it does, you are usually ok.

Which leaves us the last little percentage of bad luck, which we can reduce even further by training and planning, such as researching, planning and practicing what one will do in the moment of unexpected events or behaviours.

But, fundamentally, in the vast majority, horses are safe.

As are bicycles, aeroplanes, cars, warm seas and novelty slippers.

Chapter 3

*"He who says it cannot be done, should not
interrupt the one doing it"*

Chinese Proverb

Congratulations! You've made it to the inevitable conclusion where we start our journey, a conclusion which many riders don't get to. It's an important step for our subconscious, and to our view of the world.

It's possible.

It's possible.

Don't think of a Frog

Watch out for the people you spend your horse-time with.

They don't like this kind of talk – that horses are safe, that they're getting safer, that we already have the abilities to cope.

Why don't they like it? Because it's placing the responsibility for taking action firmly back in their own hands.

They don't like this kind of talk because it leaves the blame of fear firmly at the feet of the rider, not the horse or the conditions.

This kind of talk is saying, "You can do what you want to do, you just won't." And that's a tough lesson to hear!

In fact, it's so true, that I think I'll put it down again.

You CAN do what you want to do.

In its own way, that statement is more frightening than any horse behaviour.

It's even possible that the people surrounding you may wish to *intentionally* reside in their fears and anxieties.

That because their fears and anxieties what they're used to, - or even part of their self-image. There's a strange kind of comfort, in the proudly stated assumption that they are doing all they can, and circumstances beyond their control are thwarting their abilities.

"There is nothing I can do. The horse senses my adrenaline."

In addition, their trials and tribulations attract support and welcome words from their network of associates, and that's comforting, too.

They may even be portrayed as, - or portray themselves as - the struggling under-hero, giving their best in the face of adversity. Rather than take responsibility, (and action), it's far more comforting to agree that horse riding is the most dangerous sport there is, and it is OK to feel scared. "We all do", they'll say.

Fear. Is it real? Or is it imagined?

But we now know that danger is not the same as fear. Danger is real, and assessable to all. Fear is imaginary, and subjective………….and infectious!

You might be feeling very confident when you go down the yard, maybe you've read a few chapters of this book, maybe you watched Hidalgo on the telly last night, and you're feeling enjoyably confident going out on your horse.

As soon as you're at the yard, you're tacking up, looking forward to your ride, and Candice is tacking up her horse as well to come out with you. You're happily tacking up, tightening girths and generally enjoying the sunshine and the smell of leather. You're already looking forward to your ride.

However, you've not yet even mounted up before Candice is already cautioning you against HER forthcoming fears.

"It is bin day."

"It is a bit windy."

"Let's not go on the lower road"

…or whatever. Whittling away at *your* confidence, because *Candice* is frightened. And if Candice is persistent enough, you'll find your confidence fading away.

Is this sounding familiar?

So if you persist on going on your ride, on feeling confident, and despite Candice's protestations you do go out along the lower road. You will, without doubt, find that Candice is reminding you that around this corner is a farmhouse which puts the bins out on a Wednesday.

You can be most certain that Candice will ensure that you are not only aware of, but positively anticipating and expecting the potential dangers of this bin at least 500 yards before you get to it.

"Don't forget there's a bin along here, it's just along here, is just around this corner, the bin, if Rocky jumps at the bin, make sure that the bin the bin the bin the bin the bin."

"There was a woman in Patagonia who's horse jumped at a bin and her head came off………."

By the time you actually get to the bin, and Rocky actually sees the bin, Candice has been ensuring that YOU are appropriately apprehensive of the bin, and have been for at least the last five minutes. Candice has been building her own anxiety about the bin ever since you were tacking up on the yard, half an hour ago! Finally Rocky sees the bin, and he doesn't like bins, so Rocky is spooking at the bin, Candice is spooking at the bin, you are spooking at the bin, ……….

What hope has your steady old Nelson got of ignoring the bin and going for a lovely extended trot up the farmer's track to the beautiful spot where you'd like to have a canter and admire the wonderful view? Three of the four brains staring fixedly at a bin! If there was a manual as to How To Train Your Horse To Be Scared Of Bins, this would be it.

Instead of putting all your concentration into what you DON'T want, like bins, there is always the alternative: to consider what you DO want – and *not* think about what you *don't* want. Do we want to walk around country lanes, from bin to bin staring fixedly at each one? Do we say "Let's go for a ride! Let's go stare at some bins!"

……..Or do we want to go for a lovely extended trot up the farmer's track to the beautiful spot where you'd like to have a canter and admire the wonderful view?

Let's just digress for a second to try a quick technique which I call Don't Think Of A Frog.

I am going to count down from 3, and when I get to Zero, I would like you to NOT think of a frog.

Ready ?

Three, two, one……

…. And of course you are thinking of a frog.

OK then, think of a frog if you must but just make sure it is not a blue and pink striped one!

You see? It's impossible!

My (and my froggy friend) are making the point that, if you decide to concentrate on what you DON'T want, ("I don't want to have problems at the bin") …you are producing a picture of that outcome quite firmly in your mind, which will duly be sent for processing to your subconscious. And your subconscious will duly respond with ideas, dreams, behaviours and inspirations, to make sure you get exactly what you ordered.

Here's a splendid elucidation of that principle. I remember once that a lady came to me for one to one hypnotherapy. As part of our initial consultation, I asked her, "What DO you want to ride like?"

She immediately replied with what she DIDN'T want to ride like - "I just want to ride with enough confidence that I'm not shaking in the saddle, trembling and singing the lead song from Frozen."

So what picture did she have in her mind?

"*Let it go / let it go /………..* "

It took quite a while for her to allow herself to describe – and overcome quite a lot of resistance to visualising - what she DID want to ride like.

And it turns out, that she wanted to ride like her friend, who rode with the principle that she would Hope for the Best and Deal with the Rest, who rode with enough confidence to know that the horse will not behave 100% perfectly all the time, and this is perfectly normal for a horse. However, no matter what happened, she was the person to deal with it, calmly, efficiently and safely, and get on with enjoying her horses.

Our horses aren't going to be perfect. Life's not like that, and horses certainly aren't! The thing to realise is, it doesn't matter what your horse does, it's how you react that matters.

That's worth saying again.

<u>It doesn't matter what your horse does, it only matters how you react.</u>

Dealing with Danger

So what is it, in our minds that allows us to encompass the complexities of driving, riding bicycles, swimming and crossing the street, but won't allow us to encompass the complexities of horse riding?

Well, this is where I go back to my previous life as a hypnotherapist.

I grew up in the 70's …. Uri Geller was bending his spoons and reading minds, hypnosis was the buzzword around our school. I was going to make my money by going into banks with a pendulum and hypnotic stare …..

It didn't quite work out like that.

Nonetheless, I dabbled in sports hypnosis and gradually became specialised in rider confidence, then as my Rider Confidence Course developed, I thought perhaps I should go and get properly qualified. So I went along to the Clifton Practice, the largest Hypnotherapy College in the South West, and enrolled in a course in Solution Focused Hypnotherapy, which was great fun and simply fascinating. For a while, I entered the world of mainstream clinical hypnotherapy, treating anxiety, stress, depression and suchlike, smoking, weight loss, all the usual stuff. And I really really enjoyed it.

But gradually, my list of Rider Confidence clients grew and grew, and nowadays I pretty much exclusively only include hypnotherapy principles and practice in my Rider Confidence courses, books and internet based programmes and platforms. (www.karlgreenwood.co.uk)

However, what I learnt in those days, and the experiences I had as a clinical hypnotherapist has a great relevance to the Rider Confidence programmes I run today - so if you'll allow me, I will take a few moments to explain what is going on in our brain, and why our minds work the way they do.

Chapter 4

The Marvellous Problem-Solving Brain

Here is a picture of a brain.

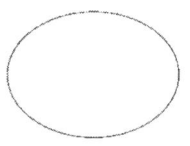

It is not to scale or anatomically correct, but a brain it is none the less. This is the primitive brain shared by all animals - dogs, cats, monkeys, giraffes & horses, and it pretty much does nothing at all. It has no logic, no reason, no language, no imagination. It just sits there, scanning for danger - but unless danger threatens, it quite happily whiles away it's time, grazing on the hillside, and brushing away the flies.

If danger does threaten, or, crucially, the *perception* of danger threatens, then the primitive brain will respond with some Emergency Drills, or perhaps a better analogy would be Survival Strategies.

Survival Strategies

1) Anxiety

One of these survival strategies is anxiety. Anxiety is a fairly simple survival strategy to understand - if there are lions and tigers and bears behind every tree and bush, it pays to be not too far from your panic button.

2) Anger

Another survival strategy that it may use is anger. Again, anger is fairly easy to explain. It makes you stronger than usual, more impervious to pain, more likely to win a fight. Easy.

3) Depression

A third survival strategy that your primitive brain might use, is depression.

I was surprised to learn that depression is a survival strategy, until it was explained thus….

If we are living in our primitive society in our caves, and conditions outside are simply too bad, too cumulatively insurmountable - maybe there's an ice age going on - then it does no good at all to feel all positive and say, "Don't worry! I'll go catch a rabbit!" …. And out you go, into the snowstorm, never to be seen again. And when they dig you up in six thousand years, and analyse the contents of your stomach, guess what?

No rabbits.

No, it does us no good then to be positive at all. So we are hard wired to do the opposite. And what is the opposite of positive?

Negative. When it all gets too much, we feel negative.

When conditions are just too rough, too insurmountable, our brains take action for us. We get depressed. We don't feel like wasting energy. We certainly don't feel like, say, playing. We don't feel like getting up, we don't feel like interacting with the other members of our clan, we don't feel like cleaning the cave, we don't feel like doing anything much. We just pull the mammoth skin over our heads, and wait for better times. When the snowstorm lifts, the depression lifts, and we go and get on with our lives quite happily.

This is how it's *supposed* to work. When conditions lift, the depression lifts. If I was in charge of evolution, I would somehow make depression feel like a lovely warm hug, but I suppose my brain knows what it's doing, and instead it feels like the horrendous feeling that it does – the opposite of positive that robs us of all inclination to improve our lot – and stops us running off into the snowstorm.

When the snowstorm lifts, the depression lifts.

So why do humans get stuck in a rut then? Why doesn't depression lift? What's the problem? The problem is that evolution went on - giraffes got big long necks, baboons got bright red bottoms, and we got the short straw, all we got was a vastly augmented intellectual capability. The cerebral cortex – the seat of the Intellectual Brain. The intellectual part of our brain is nothing less than a Problem Solving Factory. This is the outer layer of our brain that looks like a big ball of wiggly worms.

Subconscious Intellectual

A.K.A. "The Problem Solving Factory"

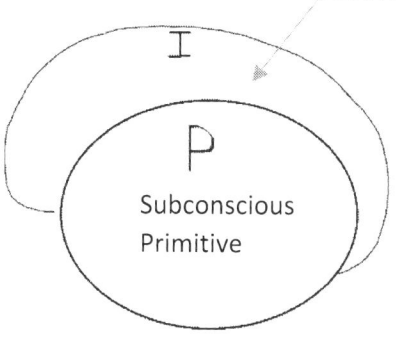

I

P

Subconscious Primitive

I = Intellectual

P = Primitive

    This Intellectual part of the brain is where imagination lives. This is also where logic lives, plus reason, language, and the seat of an intelligence that made us the most successful species ever to be seen. (Except for ants. Ants are going to take over the world. Mark my words. But that is another tale for another day.)

    The Intellectual part of the brain is a great big super effective Problem Solving Factory. Solving problems is what makes us human. It loves to solve problems. It lives for solving problems. We love it. We can't get enough of it. Achievement just feels so great. So much so that the Times crossword has even got its own fan club! Puzzle books are a multi-million-pound industry, and adolescent boys all over the country are locking themselves in their room, getting addicted to computer games spending sleepless nights and their father's credit card just for the buzz of moving from level 20 to level 21.

Humans *love* solving problems.

Whenever you achieve a success, you are rewarded with a lovely feeling of pride and self-worth, encouraging you to find more successes and overcome more problems. This feel-good factor is caused by a release of endorphins – chemicals in the brain which produce very pleasant sensations to which we attribute words like success, joy and pride. In your pottery class, should you finally managed to master the Potter's Wheel, making a vase which does NOT collapse as it goes into the kiln, but still has the characteristic vase shape as it comes out, well, this is, quite rightly, a source of pride. You show it to your friends - "Look what I made! Look what I did! Isn't it amazing?" (Well, not *too* much showing off - maybe we will just put it on the little table in the hall, where everybody can see it when they come through the front door.

We wouldn't want to appear ostentatious.)

None the less, this rush of endorphins, which so delightfully rewards a success, is what drives us forward.

In order to solve problems, we need a thing called Imagination. And what Imagination does is, *it allows us to see the results before it actually happened.*

You do not have to physically build a chair out of ice in order to know that in a temperate climate, it is not a good idea. And already you can see in your mind, a picture of somebody sitting on the floor in a puddle.

You do not have to build the chair out of Plasticine in order to see………. and already you can see the image of the result in your mind. Let's think. Something a bit more robust than Plasticine or water……..I know! You could make it out of *bricks*! That would work. And already, in our minds, is a picture of a structure that would be usable as a chair, but, in all honesty, would be better suited as a barbecue. Just like that, easy as pie. That is the power of an imagination.

Our Intellectual Brain, that is, our Problem Solving Factory, is *so* sharp, that it must be treated with caution, lest we cut ourselves. We are *so* clever, *so* imaginative, that we think almost nothing of it.

Nonetheless, it is simply amazing. You may be under the impression that your dog is pretty smart, but compared to your cerebral cortex, well, it's no contest. Fido may seem clever, but try just giving him a long stick, and call him through a doorway. Most people would not have a problem with that particular puzzle - no effort at all, without even realising that co-ordinating a stick through a door requires the most amazing imaginative and anticipatory mental processes that would confound our cleverest animal neighbours.

The key is imagination, and we are so phenomenally good at it, that we sometimes become complacent with its power. But more on that later.

So, we have our super powerful Imagination, and we have our Problem Solving Factory.

This is the way it's supposed to work:-

At the front of your Problem Solving Factory is a smaller area of your brain, which is under your conscious control. This is the boss of the factory. This is where your idea of "you" lives.

I'll just draw you in here. Again, not anatomically correct, but I have tried to be as flattering as possible.

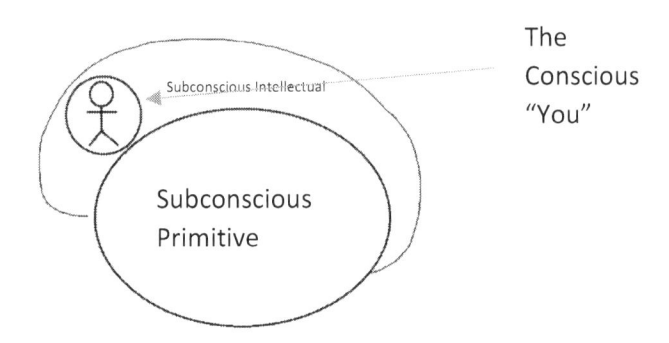

[Diagram: A stick figure labeled "Subconscious Intellectual" inside a brain-shaped outline, with a larger oval labeled "Subconscious Primitive" and an arrow pointing to the stick figure labeled "The Conscious 'You'"]

You may have heard that we only use 10% of our brains, (or 20% of our brains, or any percentage of our brains that the orators of that particular anecdote care to make up), the point is, that it is the *smaller* part of our Problem Solving Factory is under our conscious control.

So this is how it works.

The Boss of The Problem Solving Factory (the smaller, "conscious" area at the front of your brain), says to the Factory Floor (the Subconscious Intellectual), "Today's problem is - I would like to work out how I can go on a horse riding holiday around Mongolia."

The conscious Boss put the order for a horse riding holiday around Mongolia into the subconscious Problem Solving Factory.

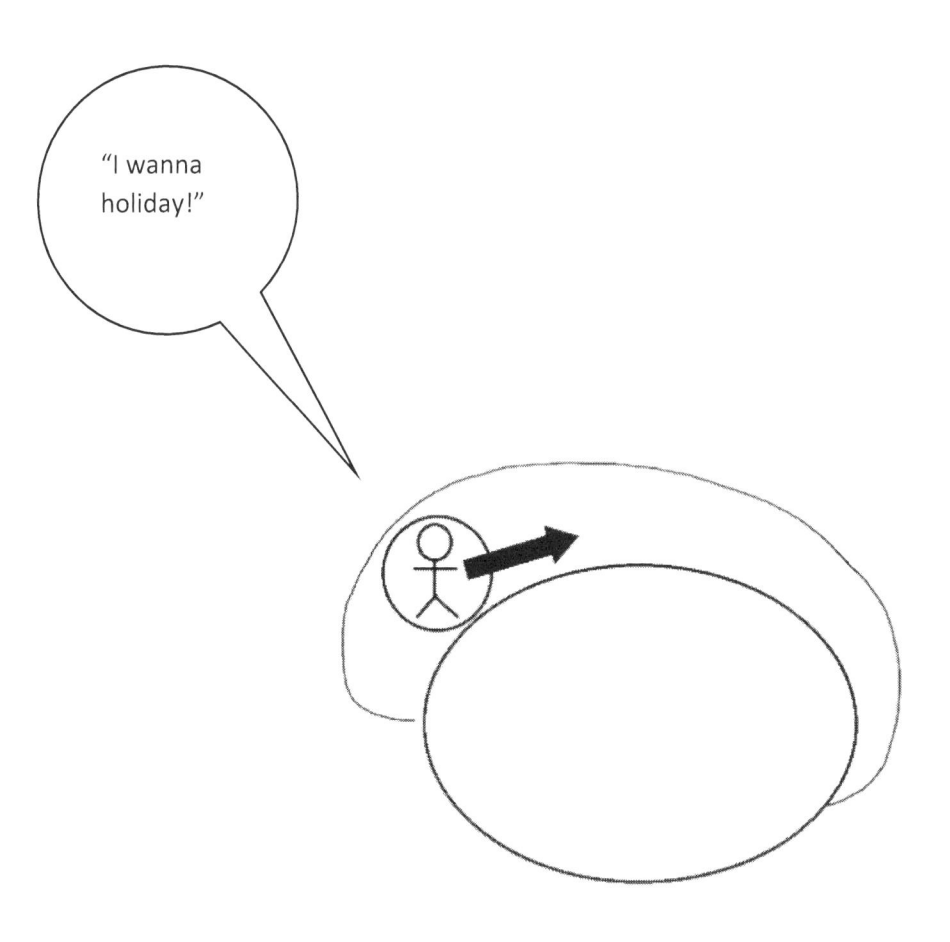

"I wanna holiday!"

How does the Boss put the order for a horse riding holiday around Mongolia into the subconscious Problem Solving Factory? By using Imagination, through a process called visualisation. The more *often* we visualise, AND the more *detail* we visualise with, the more the order goes into our Problem Solving Factory.

Let's get on with visualising my dream Mongolian holiday then.

If I close my eyes, and concentrate…….

I can see it now.

I am in Mongolia. I can see myself, on the steppes, hills sliding past in the distance, as I gallop along the grassy plain on those funny little horses. I can smell the grass. There's chickens, and goats, and horses and………

Oh yeah.

…….and the cold wind blows past my fur coat, howling past my hooded ears. There's yurts, and red-faced children in big furry hats. I am wearing a silk cummerbund, that flows behind me like a flag in the wind.

Oh, I can see it now.

The more vividly I see it, the more detailed I see it, and the more frequently I see it, the more strongly the order for a horse riding holiday in Mongolia is put to the factory floor of my Problem Solving Factory.

The order to work out how to be horse riding in Mongolia is duly received by the Problem Solving Factory, and my Problem Solving Factory gets to work by supplying me with dreams, ideas, behaviours and inspirations to help me get what I want.

Out of nowhere, my subconscious finds a dream, idea, behaviour or inspiration to get me what I want, (in this case, a holiday horse riding in Mongolia.) In the diagram below, this is shown as an arrow bringing a subconscious element to my conscious awareness.

Subconscious element making it's way to your conscious mind

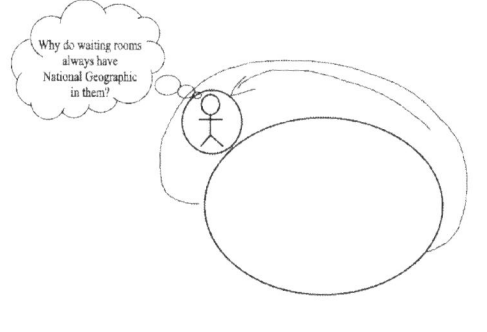

Why do waiting rooms always have National Geographic in them?

What is this element? Well, it could be anything my subconscious feels would be useful to achieve my goal. For example, I'm sitting in the dentist, lazily flicking through some back copies of National Geographic, and, blow me down, there is an article all about going on horse riding holidays around Asia!

Wow! *What* a coincidence!

I may not be actually thinking about my holiday – in this example, I'm wondering about the choice of magazine in the dentist waiting room. And out of nowhere, my subconscious sends its message – "Look here! Is this of use?"

Here comes another one. I am walking down the street, a street I have walked down a million times before, and there, on the wall, is a brass plaque, saying here is where you come to get your visa, or your jabs for Asia, or whatever. What a coincidence!

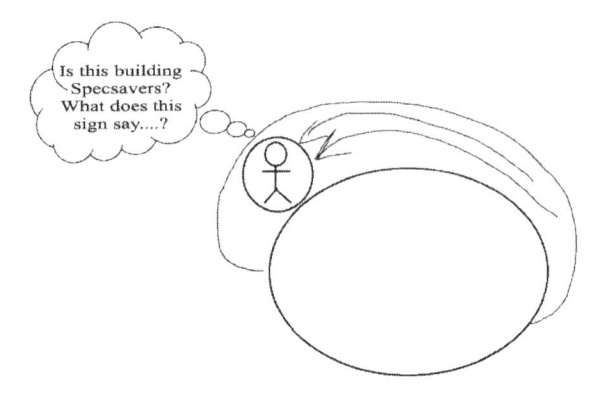

Here comes another one - I'm sitting at home, eating my beans on toast, and suddenly I think," Of course! Auntie Edna! She works in Abu Dhabi! In finance!"

She gets loads of air miles! She's always saying she doesn't know what to do with them! AND she's got loads of money! We could do a deal..."

And before you know it, I'm riding around Mongolia, with Auntie Edna, on those crazy little ponies, having a great time.

Boom.

That is how my Problem Solving Factory works.

Have you ever noticed that thing when you get a new car, and suddenly that type of car is everywhere, and you're not sure if there's an unwritten Owner's Club rule that you should flash your headlights and wave? That is a classic example of your Problem Solving Factory at work. Your subconscious constantly scanning for items that you might find useful in your quest and pushing them onto your conscious agenda for your consideration.

The *Obedient* Problem Solving Factory

However, the brain is a very faithful Problem Solving Factory. Whatever you ask for, is what you will get.

Whatever you imagine, is what your brain will do everything in its power, to give you.

Whatever you visualise.

Positive or negative.

So let's take a negative example. Something very simple. A child goes to a new school, and doesn't want to be there, so sits in the corner of the playground, crying.

The teacher goes over, and says," Small child! Why are you crying?"

"Nobody wants to play with me ", replies the child.

"Well," says the teacher. "Maybe that is because you are sat on your own, blowing snot down your top lip, and looking miserable."

So what happened?

The child was determined not to enjoy the new school, and visualised how miserable it would be. The Problem Solving Factory received the order to have a miserable time at school, and came back with behaviours, ideas, and inspiration, to get exactly what was ordered. Sit in the corner, blow snot down your top lip, and there we have it.

However, we are not children, and our brains would not *dream* of behaving in such a childish manner.

Would they?

Let's get back to horses.

We are now going to put a negative horse experience into our Problem Solving Factory. Here we go

I am closing my eyes and visualising now.

Let's see.

"I will never be good at riding horses."

"I am a terrible horse rider."

"I will *always* be a terrible horse rider."

"I will get hurt riding horses."

"I will hurt the horse! I do not deserve this horse. This horse was a good horse when I got it, now it is a terrible horse. I will fall off, fall over, and the encounter disaster every time I ride."

"All my friends know I am a terrible rider. I have no status on the yard. They all talk about me behind my back. They call me all the gear and no idea."

"My instructor is taking my money, and knows I will always be terrible. I will get hurt, the horse will get hurt, it's a waste of time, and a waste of money. My family is correct. I am wasting away our fortune. I will get hurt, and I am not capable of making things any other way."

"My horse hates me."

Please feel free to add in any more that I may have missed!

Wow! Great visualisation, folks!

········· And what the Problem Solving Factory gets asked for, the Problem Solving Factory will do it's very best to get, - with dreams, ideas, inspirations and behaviours to make sure I get what was ordered.

Here comes one dream, idea, inspiration or behaviour now.

When you wake up in the morning, you may not feel like rushing headlong towards this future of misery that you have painted for yourself. You may not feel like leaping out of bed and rushing immediately to the car. You may feel kind of down, and maybe have an extra cup of coffee, before getting in your car and going to the stables. And when you get to the stables, instead of cracking on with it in a workmanlike manner, you may just find Candice, and commiserate.

" I'm not really feeling it today…...."

You may not work to the best of your ability, and now you're late, and there isn't really time to ride anyway, so you change your mind.

"Oh dear. I am short of time. Tell you what. I will just change its rug, throw it out, and ride it tomorrow.

"But of course, this horse will be even hotter tomorrow, so maybe I will just lunge it. That's it. I will lunge it tomorrow, and ride it the next day.

"But then, it will be *four* days since I last rode it, and I did say I was going to ride it 3 times a week, and then it's my lesson, and my instructor will know that I have not ridden it, and she will gossip with all the other liveries, and they all know that I don't deserve this horse, and that I'm going to harm this horse, it will become uncontrollable, and I will get hurt…….."

Boom! There we are. But the worst isn't even over yet! Whilst you are setting yourself up to fail, your primitive brain is receiving lots of pictures of you falling, harming the horse, losing your status, arguing with your family, and having a generally miserable time. "Oh my word", it says to itself, "Conditions are rough. We are under attack, there is danger everywhere. And when we perceive danger, then it must be time to bring out the big guns, Anger, Anxiety, and of course, Depression."

Would any of this be sounding familiar, by any chance?

Compare *this* behaviour to someone who is expecting successes with their horses, - maybe they're doing well in their competitions or whatever – by the time you rock up down the stables, they are on their third horse, cheeringly circling and waving enthusiastically, calling, "Morning!"

What's the difference between you and her? You are both doing the same activity, on the same animals, with the same amount of arms and legs. So why such a different outcome?

The difference is that *your* expectations of the future are painted as a woeful struggle, and *her* expectations of the future is painted as a successful competitor – with all the social status that brings.

And that's the only difference. Your outlook and expectations.

So what's the solution?

The solution is very simple.

Watch. Your. Thoughts.

Chapter 5

Deliberate Thinking

"The thoughts you allow to take seed in your mind are the ones which will grow and take over the garden"

It is incredibly important to be aware your thoughts, and to carefully select which ones you allow to take root. For example, you are able to imagine that tomorrow is going to be a good day. *Or* you are able imagine that tomorrow is going to be a bad day. What is impossible to imagine is that tomorrow is going to be both good day AND a bad day. You *have* to choose one or the other. One choice is helpful, and one choice is destructive.

So choose the helpful one!

Our cheery friend circling on her third horse of the morning did.

It's very easy to say, isn't it? Choose helpful and positive thoughts. But I know what you're thinking….. "Yes, we all know about positive thinking, but the trouble is, negative thoughts just pop up all on their own!"

Well, yes, that's true. They do just pop up on their own. But then, all *sorts* of thoughts pop up on their own. Like scrolling through a Facebook newsfeed of life's possibilities, your moments of reverie are filled with a constant stream of speculative thoughts, nonsense thoughts, random thoughts and transient thoughts. It's the ones that *you capture and add value to* which are the ones which will become meaningful to you. Just as confidence isn't the absence of adrenaline, *deliberate* thinking isn't the absence of negative thoughts. You can and do operate exactly as you wish in the presence of negative thoughts and adrenaline – it's only when you stop and focus on that adrenaline or on that negative visualisation that YOU ATTRACT MORE OF THE SAME. The choice as to what you focus on is up to you.

Your mind is filled with a constant dribble of random thoughts. That's not an insult, by the way! All of us are like that. "That cloud looks a bit like a poodle." "If I did a world record bath of baked beans, would any of the baked beans go up my bum? " "Could I do advanced dressage lessons?" " If I was in the shower, and the house caught fire, would I be alright?" "Will I get hurt on this horse because I'm me?" "? Should I have the dead skin nibbled off my toes by little fish? "

All of these thoughts are throw away-able and dismissible, or keep-able and growable. It's your choice. Those that you deliberately choose to keep and pay attention to, allowed to take root, will be the ones that grow.

Be VERY deliberate as to which thoughts you feed and grow. Only allow those thoughts to take root, which are solely the ones that you wish to be there, for a valid and deliberate reason.

Put a bouncer on the door of your mind. Examine which thoughts, ideas, dreams and inspirations you wish to grow, and be very deliberate in only allowing beneficial ideas to access your creative genius mind.

If its name ain't on the list, it's not coming in.

The Opposite of Success is Learning.

There are some simple, effective mental tools to help you grow helpful thoughts and wither unhelpful ones. One great tool is to realise that **the opposite of success is learning**! You either succeed at something, or you learn how not to do it. There's a great story about the inventor Thomas Edison, who was asked by a reporter how it felt to have over a thousand fails at inventing an efficient, safe electric lightbulb.

"I haven't had a thousand failures" replied the inventor. "I haven't had one failure. I have had a thousand successes in learning ways in which it won't work."

And then the light bulb was finally figured out. This story, as simple as its message is, still reminds us that there is always another way to look at the world.

You either succeed at something, or you learn how not to do it. There is, therefore, no such thing as failure.

We'll come back to this in a moment, so for now, hold on to that thought.

The opposite of success is learning.

Bite Sizes.

Another great tool, is bitesizes. If you can jump an ankle-high jump, but you cannot jump a head-high jump, then have simply not done the correct bite sizes to build up to that.

And sometimes the bite size is much smaller than you would believe, but without consciously thinking of and planning what bite sizes we need, we set ourselves up to become overwhelmed.

It's even possible that our feeling of being overwhelmed is a deliberate ploy by our subconscious to prove the miserable future we have visualised for ourselves. We set out to prove we are inadequate or incapable, and refuse to break down the exercise we are trying to do into manageable chunks, and instead view the exercise as an ultimate test which we are set to fail.

People who are set to succeed, instead of set to punish themselves, are quite aware that the foundations must be set and apply those foundation steps with no emotional content. Success with horses is never linear, and follows the ups and downs of any growth chart. To keep the general trend upward, sometimes one must go back a few steps.

It is not failure to go back a few steps – it's good horse sense. Every expert regularly returns to the basics.

You would never chastise a child for wanted to master an earlier lesson – and our primitive minds operate at around the six or seven year old mark. That's just how it is and we must behave accordingly, and not be harsh on ourselves when choosing our bite size.

For example, if someone is having great success in their riding, like that lady who is on her 3rd horse, cheerily calling" Morning!", as you rock up down the stables, full of caffeine and misery, her bite size was to ride – the ride either full of success or full of learning – but to be on that horse three times a week at the minimum. In order to do that, her next bite size down would have been to ensure she was at the stables at six thirty every morning. In order to do that, her next bite size down would have been to ensure she was able to leave the house at ten past six. Ultimately, her first bite size was to *make the decision!* And the second bite size may have been something as small as gathering her family six months ago, and timetabling exactly what duties and chores each member of the family has to do when in order to allow her to leave the house on time, every day, to do her training. This simple act of making a rota and timetabling ensures that she can get out of the house at 6:10 exactly to get to the stables on time – and so she is in with a good chance to achieve her riding dreams.

One Sunday, back in February, she timetabled. That was her bitesize, and without it life would have been that much more difficult.

It's interesting to note that most of her bite sizes in the process were nothing to do with the behaviour of her horse, and everything to do with her behaviour as a horseperson.

And with that in mind, success is just a matter of choice – not fate.

Isn't that good to know?

Just with these two supertools – The Opposite of Success is Learning and choosing sensible Bite Sizes, you can pave the path to inevitable success.

Let's give an example.

Let's say, you've got a horse which you'd like to get to trot a perfect circle.

So far, either the speed, tempo or curve of the circle has been inconsistent and you're starting to wonder if it'll ever get there. Maybe it was Scary Corner, (doesn't every arena have a scary corner?), maybe distractions, maybe awkward habits which seem engrained in your horse, or possibly your horse is just having a good time at your expense – who knows?

Now there's two ways to get a horse to go in a circle. One way is to get a load of whips and ropes and mediaeval devices and force it to go in a circle.

The other way is to be like the role model horseperson we wish to be, to emulate our inspirations and act as the best horsepeople do – never getting upset, never getting angry, never getting depressed but instead endeavouring to learn the causes and trying out possible solutions with a sense of humour and patience.

(I'm hoping you'd like to be included in the second example and not the first. If you are in the first method, perhaps this section isn't for you!).

So here we are, trying to understand how to get our horse to go in a circle, and being the horseperson we wish to be, with a sense of humour and patience.

Your helpful instructor comes up one day, and offers you an aid to try – the latest craze in the horsey community.

"Have you seen these? They're called Uber-Straps. Everyone's using them these days, I think it's worth a try with your horse!"

You take the advice, take the Uber-Strap, and give it a try.

However, before you head out to the school, you remind yourself of the bite sizes of the day. Our *exercise* today is to test out the Uber Strap. Our *bite sizes* today are:

1) Remember to either succeed, or learn, or both
2) Not get angry
3) Not get upset
4) Not get depressed
5) Learn how the Uberstrap can help.
6) Operate with a sense of humour and patience.

Notice how all of the targets above are independent of your horse's behaviour. That's fantastic – you can't fail!

Unless you choose to, of course.

So we're going to test the Uberstrap.

We head out to the school.

We set everything up, and test the Uberstrap on say, setting number 4, somewhere in the middle, and set our horse off to complete its circles.

The circles are as bad as ever.

We take off the Uber-strap, change the adjustment from hole number 4, and try hole number 2.

The circles are, if anything, worse.

"Aha!" we declare. "Now I'm learning!" We set the Uberstrap on hole number 6.

"Watch this."

The circles are worse.

And there you have it. End of the exercise, and now to have a little look back over the session and take what value it offers.

So, what have we learned? We have learned:

That the Uberstrap is rubbish.

That our instructor is fallible.

That this horse isn't matched to that type of aid.

So have we succeeded?

YES!

Remember, what was the point of the exercise? The point of the exercise was to try the Uberstrap, succeed OR learn, but, most of all, to be like the horseperson we want to be – that is, succeeding or learning without getting, angry, upset or depressed.

And that we did!

So to all the other yard users, leaning on the fence to judge your work instead of getting on their own horses, you've just gone out and done the worst circles for six months, yet come back in triumphant and beaming!

Well done you. THAT is the bite size you need to master to move on.

Be kind to yourself, and break your bite sizes down into easy chunks.

"But!" I hear you cry – "What about my circles?"

Well, I'm sorry but I don't know. There's all sorts of reasons, further compounded by the fact that the horse, the school and the Uberstrap are all imaginary, but what I do know, is that the solution begins with a horsepersons attitude of learning, instead of getting upset.

Imagine a room full of astro-physicists, studying the rotation of the planets and stars. Would you expect to find them crying and screaming "I don't know why Mars won't go in a circle! Why does this have to happen to me? Oh god I'm so pointless!"

Of course not. The astro-physicists study the causes, suggest answers and patiently trial solutions.

It's worth saying one more time –

The Opposite of Success is Learning.

De-valuing Unhelpful Negative thoughts.

So how can you make sure that you view your negatives thoughts without any value when they DO arise? Negative thoughts, like all thoughts, pop up on their own and before you know it you're giving them your attention.

So what can we do at that point to rob them of their value?

One technique I use to rob my negative thoughts of their value, is to view them with humour.

Let me give an example - I have one particular negative thought, happens to me all the time, - maybe it happens to you - when I'm driving down the road, with the weight of the world heavy upon my shoulders, and the sun is setting in a beautiful sunset, golden light somehow bathing the clouds in pink, painting the world in deep, rich warmth.

And the little negative thought pops up, "Wouldn't it be nice to drive on - into the sunset. Just keep driving? Simply drive off, away from the stresses of life? 'And they rode into the sunset for a life happily ever after.' Wouldn't that be lovely? Just drive away………"

Of course, if I *did* drive into the sunset, by the time the sun set, I would be in Swindon.

That would be awful!

And there we are.

With a little bit of humour, the negative thought is robbed of all its value. (And an apology issued to all the people of Swindon, it's a lovely town.)

You can view your negative thoughts with humour, or, equally useful, you can view your negative thoughts with interest. It's worth repeating. You can view negative thoughts with humour, you can view them with interest. What you *don't* do is give them any value and allow them to take root. Every thought that is in your head is in their because you have *deliberately* invited it to stay.

Living in the world of deliberate thinking, is a bit like moving to another country. It's unfamiliar, feels a bit forced.

In fact, it is quite hard work. Unfamiliar customs, and ways of thinking of which you are not used to have to be worked at. At least at first. However, as every expat knows, after a month or two, the new ways of your new adopted country become a comfortable habit.

As you develop the adopted new way of thinking, the neurones in your brain actually grow new connections to hardwire this new behaviour into your brain. This is an energy-intensive process that requires effort. This process of growing new connections takes about 45 days, depending on how often you repeat the new behaviour.

The Primitive OR the Intellectual

For various survival reasons, Primitive and Intellectual brains are on a seesaw.

When our Primitive Brain goes up, our Intellectual Brain goes down.

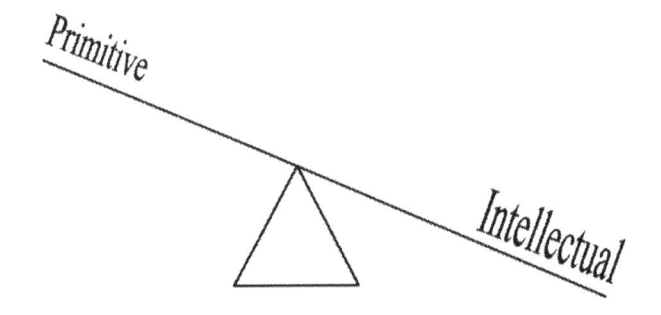

That is to say, our Primitive Brain with its fight-or-flight responses comes to the fore and implements the emergency drills to make sure we survive the situation we find ourselves in.

This is the stereotypical blind panic. The Primitive Brain over-rides the Intellectual Brain and gets us out of there!

Of course, the offset of this action is that our Intellectual Brain - the Problem Solving Factory - that makes logical, sensible decisions is supressed – leaving us to the potential of making purely instinctive actions, illogical and not necessarily sensible decisions, running around like the proverbial headless chicken.

This seesaw effect is there for a reason. It's a simple survival strategy for when danger presents itself. If a polar bear were to come through the door now, it would NOT pay to stay in my intellectual brain and think "My word! A Polar Bear! How very unusual in this temperate climate. It must have escaped from a circus. Or maybe it's a figment of my imagination. Maybe it was something I ate. It certainly looks real. I wonder if it's trained? It must be. "….Aaaaaaaand SIT!""

O no. Instead, my Primitive Mind comes to the fore and without rhyme or reason I'm outta there! On the other hand, when our *Intellectual* Brain is at the fore, our Primitive Brain is suppressed. This is when we are "In The Zone".

For example, when you are coming to the end of a project, and there's light at the end of the tunnel, and you're about to make a spectacular success - any unexpected problems that come in left-of-field, well, you're batting them off like a superhero!

Delegate this, email that, solve this crisis, email this, phone that, anticipate this, contingency that, relegate this problem or that problem and you're on the home straight!

Problems that on another day would have left you in tears are simply swept aside.

This switching from one side of the brain to the other – from the Primitive to the Intellectual, and vice versa, is a process which we are all quite accustomed to. This seesaw is a process of which we are really very recognisable. We have certainly all had plenty of experience from switching from our Intellectual Brain to our Primitive Brain. For example, you get a new phone. It's full of interesting gadgets and features. You open the instruction book determined to get this phone under your control, access all its brilliant marvels and miraculous technology. You unwrap the phone, turn it on and put your intellectual brain to work.

You're beaming at the new, shiny acquisition. "I'm just going to program my new Superphone!"

Fast forward five minutes. Yes, you know what's coming.

Enter stage left a member of your family into the room.

"How are you doing?"

You glare up from the accursed technology, face flushed with frustration and fury, eyes like coal. "I swear I am going to throw this phone across the room in a minute."

In a minute. Not only are we SO familiar with the feeling of leaving our Intellectual Brain, and going into our Primitive Brain, not only can we feel it happen when it happens, we are fully aware even before the event that we are about to undergo this process. *In a minute*, we are planning to abandon our intellectual resources, and throw the phone across the room. To be fair, I know I am exaggerating for effect, but you get the idea. (Insert your own life experiences here!)

…..AND we are quite familiar with the process going the other way as well. Going *from* the Primitive Brain into the Intellectual Brain. For example, you could be in the most *furious* of bad moods. One of those ones where nobody can help you. You are just really down and simply cannot snap out of it. SO angry! Can't even imagine a world in which fury is not the normal state of things.

All of a sudden, somebody you have been wanting to see for the last month and a half pops their head around the door." Yoo Hoo!!"

"Is now a good time?"

And your head whips up from its furious glare, and a smile drives straight through your mood and across your face. Genuine feelings of pleasure cascades through your body, as you joyfully reply," Now? A good time? Yes! Yes, of course! It's great time, come in! Come in! This vase? Yes, I made it in pottery, on the wheel no less! Oh, I know, I know.............. "

We are perfectly familiar with these processes, and it can be a source of interest to feel your mind swinging from one state to another. This interest will rob the negative mental processes of their power, as you realise what is happening. The two examples of both processes show how it is perfectly possible to take control of them, - make them happen, stop them from happening, change them for the state YOU want to be in. The choice is always yours. Ultimately, when pushed, The Boss of the Factory is always in charge.

Always. The Boss of The Problem Solving Factory – that's your idea of you, in the conscious 10% of your intellectual brain, is ALWAYS in charge, just as the boss of a factory is ultimately in charge of the factory, fire drills and emergency procedures.

Even when the polar bear strikes – if it turns out there's a baby in the path of the polar bear, you can override your emergency procedures and stop, turn around and take action. If you have to, or if you really want to.

We've covered a lot, so let's recap.

- Horses are safe.
- Horses are getting safer.
- Riding is getting safer.
- Even when it goes wrong, it's overwhelmingly fine.
- We can practice and plan for the last little percentage called Bad Luck.
- Think of what you DO want.
- Take the right Bite Sizes.
- The Opposite of Success is Learning
- The only thoughts we allow to grow are the ones we deliberately choose to.
- It doesn't matter what your horse does, it's how you react that matters.
- We can choose to be in our Intellectual Minds, regardless of adrenaline.

Wow. That is a lot!

Bucking

I'm sure you'll all agree with me that bucking is hilarious.

It's great fun.

It is! I can prove it to you - just go down to the fairground, find the bucking machine. The bucking bronco, with a fantastically long queue of people waiting to go on, knowing that they, *100-percent*, are going to get bucked off. Not only that, but they are going to PAY the man, to make *sure* they get bucked off!

Of course, I'm being facetious. Forgive me. We know that the reason the bucking bronco is fun is the knowledge that when you fall off you won't get hurt. (Probably.) However, it's worth noting that in the front of the ride is still a little sign that says," You ride this ride at your own risk."

And undoubtedly the man who runs the ride will have a story of someone who fell awkwardly and got their finger stuck in their ear and had to go to hospital. Or something.

My point is, why not learn how to fall so you won't get hurt? There are courses and internet programmes designed for this very purpose – and when did you last have a plan in place? I'll recommend my own internet programme, of course (www.karlgreenwood.co.uk) but there are others.

And when you know how to fall, you'll know you won't get hurt. Practice how to fall. On your bed, on your sofa, buy a crash mat, go to the adults' gymnastics, whatever, but have a plan in place that is practiced and automatic. And when you know exactly what you're going to do in order to not get hurt, then you will find the confidence for action you need to take control over your bucking horse.

Here at The Centre of Horseback Combat, we generally we use the policy to keep a bucking horse going forward, in order to turn the bucks into a series of jumps. And we can do jumping, so we won't fall off. The bucks where we fall are a mixture of bucking combined with stopping – so push on! And if you DO fall off – have a plan. If you plan and practice exactly what you are going to do in the event of a fall, then came the day that the horse misbehaves, instead of hanging onto the reins and gripping up, thinking " What if I fall? What if I fall? What if I fall?", - well, I KNOW what if I fall, so now I can think, lift this rein, put on that leg, do whatever is required. Which will decrease my chances of falling in the first place.

Adrenaline

I'm aware my work with horses may appear at first glance to be quite extreme, but there are simple tips which can apply to everybody which are very easy for me to share.

I am old enough to remember the days before ABS systems in car brakes, and the advice back in the day to avoid your wheels locking up during a skid was to pump the brakes repeatedly to keep the skid under control. This was advice from the rally drivers, from what may appear to be the extremes of driving, passed down to the normal car drivers in the population. So, when you are driving down a country lane in November and your car wheels skid on a patch of wet leaves and the car kicks out - your heart still leaps, adrenaline still kicks it, but you are perfectly in control in your intellectual capabilities to think "Argh! Quick, pump the brakes!".... and you go on your way. I am confident I can do that – even though I know the adrenaline will kick in. I can pump my brakes with or without adrenaline.

That's because confidence is NOT the absence of adrenaline.

We do not all float around on a Cloud of Confidence - it doesn't work like that. Confidence is the knowledge that you can stay in your Intellectual Brain and can deal with any situation irrelevant of having adrenaline in your body or not. And because we regularly do this in so many areas of life – cars, bikes, roads, and so on, it makes no sense to suppose that things should be different when we are on our horses.

The fact is that we CAN operate if adrenaline is there. Adrenaline is just a chemical that produces certain feelings – it is our choice to interpret those feelings. I am excited. I am scared. I am thrilled.

There is no point waiting for adrenaline to go away before you ride with confidence. How will you ever learn to be confident if you just avoid excitement?

The trick is to take yourself out of your comfort zone regularly and into a habit of operating with a manageable amount of nerves. Make a plan to perform your regular exercise routine, but make one small change every day – maybe one day put a bin in the arena, or tie a flag to the fence, or have a small hack out at the end – just a small change. Put all your attention into acting in the perfectly normal manner in which you acted yesterday, taking no notice at all of this new addition. In no time at all you'll be happily passing all sorts of distractions and potential spooks.

There was a great study done whereby a group of nervous horse riders were asked to hack along a hedge-line, in which there was a small gap. They were told that on the sixth pass, something would come out of the gap.

This was a lie. Nothing and no-one was going to come out of the gap, yet every horse spooked on the sixth pass.

This study shows that it is *ourselves* that we have to work on – *our* spookiness. Making small changes in our environment is for *us* to get used to flags and bins! As you de-sensitise your horse, you're also desensitizing yourself.

Make a plan. Use your imagination Have some fun with it. Get others involved. Organise bomb-proofing days. Go on other people's bomb-proofing days. You're certainly not alone in your worries, so why not help others meet those worries head on, in small, manageable bite sized bits? It might be fun…………..and horses are meant to be fun!!

Chapter 6

Stress

"I am an old man, and have known a great many troubles, but most of them never happened."

Mark Twain

      In this section we are going to look at how our brains handle stress. You will realise, of course, that this does not only apply to the stress of horses, but also that of general life – our relationships, our careers, our self-esteem. I often find that people who have completed my courses report back other benefits too – their public speaking was better, their downhill skiing was better, their violin recital was easier, they lost their worries that the car would break down. This makes perfect sense – if you are taking control of one area of your life, such as your horses, then your identity as someone who CAN take control of a situation is enhanced.

      Back to the construction of our brains. In our primitive brain, is a mechanism for dealing with stress which we can represent with a bucket. This is our stress bucket.

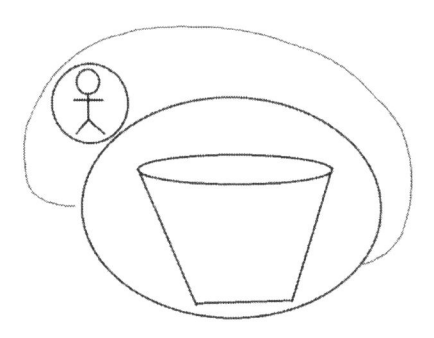

Some people have big stress buckets, some people have small stress buckets.

Into this bucket goes all the stresses of everyday life.

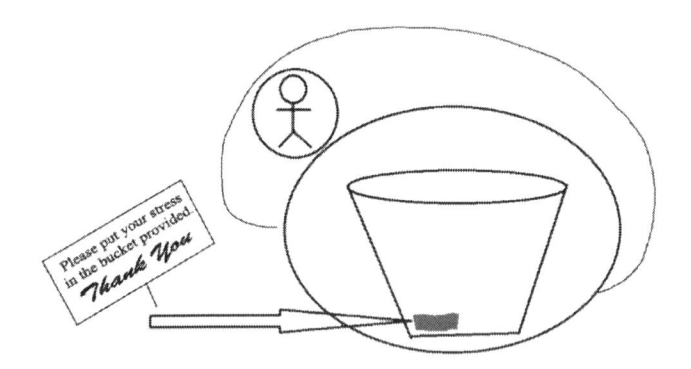

Here are some examples of some every day stresses that might occur.

- I was late to the stables.
- The horse stood on my foot.
- The car broke down.
- I had a row with my partner.
- I had to get the bus into town.
- The bus was late.
- When I got to town they did not have the things that I wanted.
- The salesman was very persuasive and sold me something else.
- When I got home the new purchase was not compatible with my equipment.

- There was a letter from the bank saying I should not have all the equipment in the first place.
- So I had another row with my partner.

What a terrible day!

All of these stresses go into your stress bucket, and if your bucket is full enough at the end of the day, you will be sat in tears with a bucket of red wine as well as a bucket of stresses!

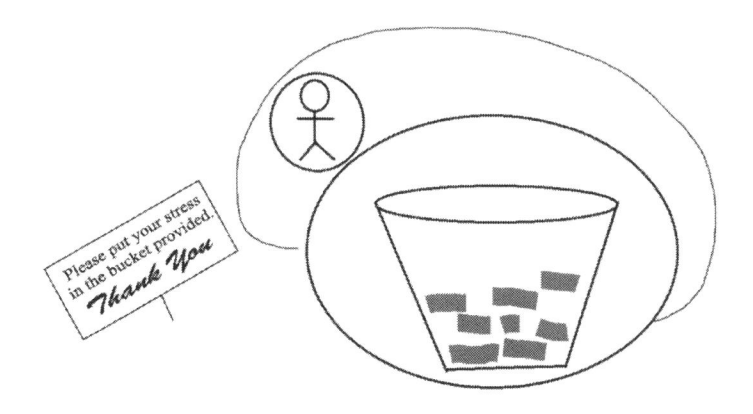

Please put your stress in the bucket provided. Thank You

How does the brain remove the stress?

Well, during the sleeping hours our brain deals with the stresses of the day.

The process of dealing with these stresses is characterized by a rapid eye movement (usually abbreviated to REM) which can be seen behind the eyelids of a dreaming person. This REM sleep is very energy intensive - it is the process of the brain taking each stress out the bucket, removing the emotional content, and then placing those stresses in the back of the brain, now converted into a narrative memory with no emotion attached. That is why the following day, we can tell the story of a day from hell without bursting into tears.

REM sleep, being very energy intensive, only lasts for 20 minutes or so, and then there is a period of deep, recuperative sleep of 90 minutes or so to rest and recover.

Then another period of REM sleep, then 90 minutes of deep sleep, then 20 minutes of REM sleep, then 90 minutes of deep sleep.

A final 20 minutes of REM sleep, and we wake up in the morning, with an empty bucket, ready to start a new day.

That is the way it's supposed to work, all in the primitive brain, which knows exactly what it's doing, and has known for hundreds of millions of years.

The problem is the young and funky Intellectual Brain, - the New Kid On The Block - with its newfangled Imagination.

For only the last 7 million years, the Intellectual Brain has been playing the movies of the what-might-be. The what-ifs. These movies are playing to a full house. There's you, your Primitive Brain, and itself, the Intellectual Brain containing your Problem Solving Factory.

Up until 7 million years ago, the only movies playing to the Primitive Brain were memories or current experiences. The pictures inside our minds are made of electrical impulses, and the electrical impulse of a memory is no difference to the electrical impulse of imagination is no different to the electrical impulses carrying information of the world around us right now. The good old Primitive Brain – who has been working in its tried and tested method for *hundreds* of millions of years - hasn't got a snowball in hell's chance of even knowing what imagination is. The Primitive Brain certainly has no way of telling imagination from memory from reality. As far as the primitive brain is concerned, every picture flying around is a representation of a real and present danger.

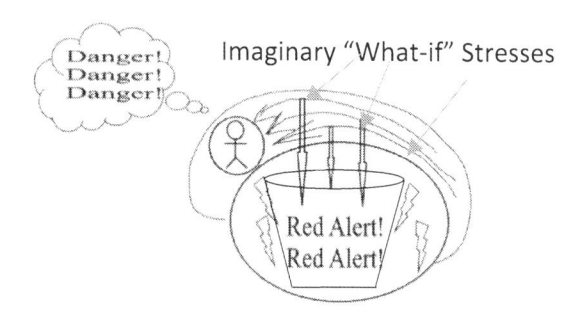

So as well as day-to-day stresses, the car, the bank, the row with your partner etc., the stress bucket in the primitive brain is also filling up with imaginary stresses. "I will always get hurt, I am damaging this horse, I have no respect on the yard, I will always do badly", etcetera etcetera.

We can see that the stress bucket is getting artificially filled up with imaginary stresses. And if you are in the habit of depressed, negative or dark thinking like this, chances are that you are in the habit of thinking in a depressed mode about *other* areas of your life as well, your family, your finances, your career, your self-esteem, your relationships and so on.

Imaginary Stresses

Real Stresses

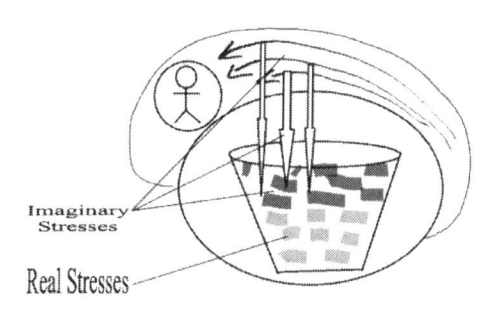

All the imaginary stress is artificially filling your bucket, and there is only a certain amount of time during the night for your REM sleep to clear away the decks. Quite possibly, by the time the morning comes, your bucket will still have some stresses in it which have not yet been dealt with. A surplus.

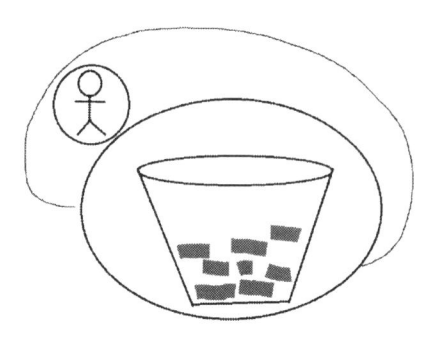

The following day your stress bucket will have new real stresses of the new day placed in it. If you allow it, new imaginary stresses will be placed in it as well.

You can see that if you continue to take a negative view of the world the surplus will grow and grow. As the days turn into weeks, the weeks turn into months, the months turn into years, years turn into decades, we see that your stress bucket will get more and more full. An artificially filled stress bucket leaves less and less room to cope with life's *actual* challenges.

And so, day after day it takes less and less extra stresses to move you into employing your Survival Strategies of Anxiety, Anger or Depression – you get a shorter and shorter fuse.

If left unchecked, your stress bucket will eventually overflow, leading to a free-flowing anxiety that has no noticeable root cause.

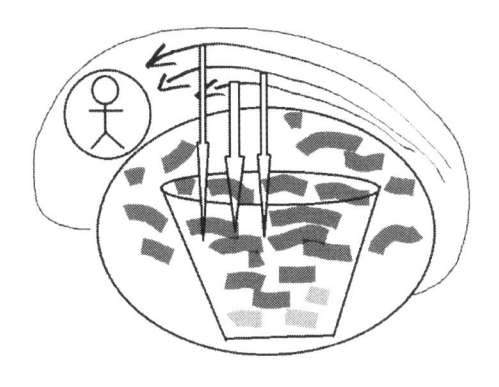

"PANIC !!!"

This is where panic attacks come from, the sudden feeling from nowhere that you are about to die, for no discernible reason at all. Or perhaps instead we will develop a sudden phobia. An overflowing stress bucket is where people might say, "I used to be fine at flying on aeroplane, now I am frightened of it." Or they might say, "I used to be *so* confident at horse riding, and now I'm terrified."

Although not exactly desirable, or enjoyable, this process of the stress bucket filling and overflowing, inducing panic attacks and phobias, is nonetheless a perfectly normal process which does tend to happen occasionally in our lives. One great example is when we have our exams as teenagers. Along with the general stress of being a teenager, this sudden stress and consequences for your future can be overwhelming. And teenagers are famous for having mood difficulties, eating disorders, anger, anxiety and depression at this time of life, are they not?

Another stereotypical time when your stress bucket will overflow is when you have kids. This is where post-natal depression come from. This is when people say," I used to be fine on my horses, then I had kids, and now I'm not. "

You can find endless examples from all areas of life - it has happened to us all.

What can we do about it, then?

The answer is simple. Too simple, if anything. Choose your thoughts *deliberately* and with care. Do the necessary work and effort to NOT allow your stress bucket with to fill with imaginary stresses – after all, MOST of the things you worry about never even happen. Be very *deliberate* as to which thoughts you allow to take root in your mind.

Most of the things you worry about never even happen.

It sounds almost too simplistic, but make no mistake, - it's work. It's work, and it's an effort. But the rewards are worth it – not only does your stress bucket empty in the sleep process, but your Problem Solving Factory has only positive orders to fulfil – and will work night and day to supply you with the dreams, ideas and inspirations to make them your reality.

"Aaaaand Sleep……."

The other thing we can do of course, is sort out as sleep patterns as best we can to allow our primitive minds the REM sleep processes it needs to empty the stress bucket.

Some of the responsibilities we have to ourselves are obvious, but I'll state them all the same. Do not drink alcohol before going to bed, (it disrupts your normal deep sleep cycle). Do not drink caffeine before going to bed. Go to bed at the same time, and get up at the same time. Do not wait until you feel tired to go to bed – stress will of course make you feel more alert and start off a cycle of poor sleep patterns. If you cannot sleep, read or listen to relaxing sessions freely available on the internet. You may or may not drop off, but you'll certainly relax and start the essential REM processes that we need – getting up and watching TV or engaging on social media certainly will not.

Taking these sensible steps will allow your normal sleep cycles to empty your bucket, and we can continue to work on which thoughts we allow to take root in our minds and prevent the stress bucket from becoming artificially filled again.

But sometimes negative thoughts feel comforting! It's a curious fact, but there is, weirdly, a certain comfort in sitting down and having a good mope. It feels comforting and familiar to have a bit of a miserable dwell. It is a bit like comfort food - we know it's not good for us but we have it anyway because we feel sad. It's a luxury.

But I must point how to get the consequences of these thought patterns can be very costly indeed. What is the COST of sitting and having a good mope, feeling sorry for ourselves or sulking? The cost is filling our stress buckets with stresses, risking a feeling of low self-esteem and low expectations. The cost is increasing our chances of hard wiring depressive thought patterns into our minds. The cost is in reducing the effectiveness of any positive thought and intent that we may have been investing in, increasing our chances of suffering from stress, anxiety, anger and depression. That's a hell of a cost for the luxury of moping.

(As an alternative, if you want to have a costly luxury, may I recommend Hawaii?)

This is how our brains work. If you want your brain to work, fill it with positive thoughts and intentions. Putting positive thoughts and intentions in a brain is the same as putting petrol in a car. If you want the car to work - put the petrol in the car. If you want your brain to work - put positive intent in your brain. It's that simple. Put the petrol, in the car.

Negative intent will not make your brain work as it should, in the same way that baked beans in the tank will not make your car work as it should.

If you want the car to go, put the petrol, in the car.

Chapter 7

Discussions

Through speaking to thousands of clients over the last decade or so, I've had some interesting and illuminating discussions with some really fabulous riders after they have been through my course on Rider Confidence, or during the chats after my talks around the country.

Our discussions regularly stray from the remit of Confidence, and into the realm of horsemanship which I am always reluctant to do. There are SO many trainers, courses and systems out there, many of which are contradictory. If one wishes to join the madding crowd of horse training opinion and method one can find oneself under attack from all sides, so generally I avoid the area as much as possible, as I can spend my time riding and having fun rather than arguing the toss about this or that training system.

Having said that, I offer below some brief points of my training philosophy and methods with which I have enjoyed a lot of success.

Teach Your Horse to Learn How To Learn

Teach your horse to learn how to learn. At the same time - as a free bonus - you can learn how to teach - how to lead.

Your horse *needs* to learn things from you. But the very *process* of learning is a process that he or she needs to learn too.

For example, if your horse needs to learn how to say, pass tractors, well that's a biggie for your horse to begin its learning on if it has never been taught how to learn ANYTHING before.

So why not spend some time teaching it how to learn? Learn what? It doesn't matter, just learn How To Learn. Learn anything and everything. Pin a poster or a feed bag on a fence and learn how to lead past that. Put a tarpaulin on the ground and learn how to walk over that. Get a Swiss exercise ball and learn how to knock that around the arena. Tap a stick on the arena fence and learn how to do that. Make up a flag and learn how to carry that. Small, big, easy, hard, useful, silly– it doesn't matter WHAT you teach the horse, it matters THAT you teach the horse SOMETHING.

The purpose of learning is to expand their, and your, comfort zone. A learning process should be out of what is comfortable and familiar, but not so far out that it is in the fear zone. A feed bag pinned to the fence at the far end of the arena is a good start, then when that is accustomed to, a second bag at the near end, building up gradually but inevitably to a complete tolerance of signs, banners and flags.

Every week, learn something new. Eventually, the process of learning becomes so automatic, that learning about tractors and bicycles, garden hoses and lawnmowers is an automatic referral to his or her teacher – that's you.

In this process, of course, you will start learning how to teach and lead. It doesn't matter WHAT you lead in, it only matters THAT you lead. In this way your position as the leader becomes automatic.

Horses like having leaders. They don't really like having to make the decisions, and anyway they are not allowed to. My horses are not looking to me to be their friend – they have their friends in the field. They are looking to me to be their leader.

Get ready for a tear-jerking story. (Don't worry – it has a happy ending!)

I once had a horse fall into a freezing ditch in winter. The temperature was well down in the minuses, there was snow on the ground and the horse had stood on some snow covered plant life at the edge of the ditch, and gently slithered in. It was balletic and serene, followed by a bout of plunging and scrabbling which ripped the lead rope out of my hand and finalised the position of the horse fully in the ditch.

What truly amazed me was the speed at which the horse abandoned all attempts to save itself and simply stood to look at me to do something. After an age of trying to persuade the horse to climb out of the ditch – which it seemed quite capable to do – I realised that the horse would stand there and die from cold rather than take the lead itself in order to save its own life.

I realised that the horse was quite right. After a lifetime of being safely led through the battlefields of BinBagLand, the World War Three of car hosepipes, mowers, bright Lycra Cyclists and trucks and dogs and Crow-Scaramageddon and whatever else, – from the horse's point of view, I had led him through so many life and death situations that I must be the one to lead him out of this one as well.

The realisation that this is what trust means is the heartbreak of this story. But it MUST be this way, for we are intelligent and can see the safe way out of a situation, taking due care of our horses, staff, riders, passers-by and ourselves.

(By the way, thank you to the farmer who kindly help extract the horse with his Manitou teleporter that winter's morning, and yes, I did have to get in it. That ditch was SOOOO cold!!!)

When I allocate horses to paddocks, I always try to have three or more horses to a paddock. This keeps the political dynamic of the field rotating, as one horse becomes dominant, the others band together and allegiances rotate, just as with people. In a two-horse relationship, one horse will become dominant and the other will become a follower. This just seems to be the natural order of things in the Politic Equus.

In our relationship with a horse, we need to make sure that it is US who are the leaders. I repeat, horses don't need us to be their friends, - they have friends in the fields. Horses need us to be strong leaders, then they'll learn how to learn and follow us anywhere.

Bolting

Bolting is a common concern. So what's actually happening when a horse bolts? It's being frightened, or it's misbehaving. Usually it is a fear response.

When a horse suddenly faces a life or death situation, such as the Wotsit packet of Death or the Pheasant of Doom, it should look to you to direct it. Think of it like this – Imagine that you are walking down a city road, and BANG! There's a huge crash, glass flying everywhere and you don't know what on earth is happening. Which would you rather have as a companion in that circumstance? Your friend, who looks at you with panic as you look at them with panic and you mutually scream,

"Aaaaaaaaarrrrggghhhhh! What's Happening???? I DON'T KNOW!! AAAAAAaaaargh!"

…….. or would you rather be with a policeman, who says, with total authority and with no shadow of a doubt, - "Get under that doorway, stay under that doorway and keep your arms over your head!"

You'd rather be with the policeman, wouldn't you? Strong, knowledgeable and authoritative. It doesn't matter if he's your friend or not, he's the one to be trusted and you'll be ok.

However, your friend cannot magically turn into policeman or a voice of authority if in the day-to-day that has not been the case. If you are authoritative with your horses from day one: -

"You will WAIT!" until I have tied up your haynet.

You will STAND! – while I wash your feet.

You will BACK! – when I enter your stable.

...that is to say, if you take the position of an authoritative leader, at every moment, in every activity – from standing still to be washed to being leading in a head collar by your side – not in front, not behind, but by your side - then when World War Three breaks out – or the Wotsit packet of Death leaps from the hedge, or the Pheasant of Doom leaps from the hedgerow - your position of authority can insist that the exercise you are engaged in continues – leading to the paddock, trotting in a circle or whatever.

Feel free to set up minor changes to take control over – such as a feed bag pinned to the arena fence, or a garden sprayer set up at one end of the arena, or carry a flag, wheel a bin into the arena, get Uncle Frank to play Pop Goes Wagner on the tuba - anything you can think of, to drive your horse on in an authoritative manner when it wants to try to take control. Small bite sizes, every day, establishing yourself as the go to authority when scary comes to town.

Don't Stop!

When the unexpected happens, the impulse is to stop, collect yourself, calm the situation and then resume the exercise. Unfortunately, a horse can rapidly learn to get out of an exercise by behaving in a manner which causes you to stop the exercise. You can see it often. A horse will be going forward, then start to shake it head or otherwise misbehave, and what does the rider do? Stops the horse, pats it and waits for composure to return before repeating the pattern. Has this ever happened to you?

A far better option is to *make the continuation of the exercise* the reassuring factor, the go-to resource to insist on composure.

By continuing the exercise, you are teaching the horse that in moments of danger (as the horse sees it), the best thing to do is to do what you're told. In effect, each time you insist on carrying on, you are re-affirming that, when World War 3 breaks out, the best thing to do is what you're told.

This lesson was provided to me by my stallion, Luminoso. He'd got into the habit of becoming increasingly excited as we walked to his field in the morning, starting to dance and then whipping round in front of his handler and rearing, stopping me in my tracks. I'd get the situation under control, calm the horse and then continue traversing the field, only to have the excitement climb again until once more we were stopped in our tracks. Over and over again, until the journey to the field became so dangerous that I could not ask my staff to do it, and I wore a hat at all times and led him in a Chifney. He continued with this behaviour.

It suddenly occurred to me that, far from being a slave to his testosterone, as I had assumed, he was actually controlling the exercise. He was training me to stop and face him off, and I was not training him to walk on.

The crucial thing was that *my* command to walk on had been changed in my mind for me into let's stop here and calm down. I was having my mind changed for me by a horse! Lumi was taking advantage of my natural impulse to stand still in order to calm the situation.

It then occurred to me, - why do I have to stand still in order to compose myself? I don't do so in any other situation. If there's a near-miss in my car, I don't have to pull over in order to take a few breaths and compose myself – I do so on the move. If I'm upset over something in the street, I continue to walk whilst I calm down.

Why am I stopping when I lead the horse in the field? From that point on I decided that, in any given situation, I will regard the resuming of the exercise as the correct moment of rest and respite – an active rest, as it were. The horse is NOT to change my mind as to the exercise at hand. This simple tip has been tremendously successful for me, and nowadays I notice all the time, riders stopping and calming their horse when it spooks or upsets, and see their minds being changed for them by their horses.

This simple change has instilled in my horses that when you're startled, the thing to do is what you're told. This has now become a running joke at my stables.

Q: What does a horse do when it's windy?

A: What it's told.

Q: What does a stallion do when it sees a mare?

A: What it's told

Q: What do horse do when there's something new in the arena?

A: What it's told.

Oh, how the long winter evenings fly past at my house.

Faking Confidence

"There was once a couple of friends setting off on a plane. One friend was confident in flying, and one friend was absolutely terrified. White faced, sweating, trembling and repeating "We're going to crash – look at the state of this plane? I can't do this.... We're going to die...." And so on and so on.

As the plane filled with the other passengers, the aerophobe got worse. Eventually a mother and her young son got onto the plane – and the young son was REALLY freaking out. Totally traumatised by the thought of going on the plane. Clearly terrified.

The mother was doing her best, but was way out of her depth.

Now, imagine that you are the aerophobic friend on that plane.

You're scared to death, and on comes this child and is sat next to you, obviously terrified. In this situation, what would you do?

Would you turn to the screaming child and scream with him, perhaps? "OH MY GOD!! YOU'RE RIGHT! WE ARE GOING TO DIE! WE'RE GOING TO CRASH AND BURN IT'S THE DEATH OF US ALL!!!!!!!"

Is that what you'd do?

No. Of course not. Then what would you do? You'd be compelled to fake it, of course. It's as if a higher authority forces you to take control of your impulses. At the very least you'd go quiet, hide your trembling hands. Maybe you'd even be able to drag up other subjects to try to distract both yourself and the child. Even force a cheery tone of voice? Maybe. My point is, that when you

HAVE to take control – when you are DETERMINED to take control - you can.

Have you ever met an unpleasant, sarcastic and generally unfriendly person, only to be informed later that he or she is a nice person really, and that they just put on a front? Well, that front works pretty well, so from my point of view they're just a mean-spirited spiteful person. Their deeper niceness doesn't make them nice to me. If you're nasty, you're nasty, and I'll leave you alone, thank you.

If someone fakes nastiness, then they behave just as a nasty person does. They are, to all intents and purposes, to the outside world, a nasty person. It's irrelevant how they are deep inside.

In exactly the same way, if someone fakes confidence, - when they HAVE to take control – when they are DETERMINED to take control - then they behave just as a confident person does. They are, to all intents and purposes, to the outside world, a confident person. It's irrelevant how they are deep inside.

How could you tell if someone that a confident person is really confident, or just good at faking it?

If you fake any emotion, then, to all the observers, it is as if you are that emotion.

To the outside world - your associates, your horse - there is no difference between faking confidence and being confident. It'll certainly be good enough to fool the children around you.

What children?

Well, the emotional, primitive brain has been estimated to have the mental age of about six or seven years old. We all know this to be true – how many times have we reacted emotionally to someone, only to have to grow up and apologise? Do we not ask to be forgiven for behaving in such a manner? – "Sorry about earlier – I was being childish" Our emotional, primitive brains are childish.

So let's fool them!

So, if you are faking confidence, WHO are you fooling?

1) Your own childish primitive mind, as per the aeroplane metaphor. In case you've forgotten, that was the story where the "higher authority" – your intellectual mind – deliberately took control. Because it had to.

2) Your childish paranoia ("I don't like to think what people think – especially those resting their elbows on the arena fence watching me work!!")

3) Any *genuine* bullying from childish others at your yard. Yes, it does happen! Even amongst adults. But it originates from resentment and jealousy, and ultimately from fear of a loss of status in the group – all characteristics of the childish primitive brain.

4) Resentment and jealousy (childish responses) at your progress – and so your rise in status - from associates who may be not progressing as you are - especially if you are seen as overtaking them!

But most importantly – the child you really want to fool is your horse itself, which has a very immature and emotional mind and would LOVE for you to be confident. Just as you can lead a child past a perceived danger with a breezy reassurance, ("That spider's more scared of you than you are of him. Those cows won't be interested in us") so your horse would love you to as well.

When a horse spooks or is insecure, what it is asking is "This is dangerous, isn't it?"

What it then *doesn't* want is an answer from you saying (through your body movements) "I don't know, Maybe? Yes? I don't know! I'm frightened! You decide!"

You wouldn't say this to a child, so don't say it to your horse.

Here's a great exercise to practice. Give it a try.

Let's imagine that you have been hired by a wealthy individual to build confidence in their daughter and her group of friends. All you have to do is exercise your horse just as you do, and the children will just watch you, every day. They've never seen a horse before, and it would be good to let them see that horses are fine and wonderful animals to work with.

At the end of each exercise session you will be given an obscenely large amount of money. Enough to retire on.

And all you have to do is ride your horse pretending to be confident.

And there is no downside. If you decide to stay in an insecure, unconfident mode of behaviour – which may be your comfort zone, even your personal identity or self-image – if you decide to show the children that horses are to be scared of, there will be no penalty, no payback - but the job will go to the next person at your yard.

How do you think you'll behave in those circumstances? With all your dreams and wishes being granted, just by *acting* confidently on your horse?

Everything you want – just pretend to be confident on your horse.

The truth is, that is the situation you are in, right now. When you acknowledge that it DOES matter that you act confidently, then ALL your dreams and wishes (at least within the realms of horse riding!) will make their way to you.

Confidence is NOT the absence of Adrenaline

Nerves say they are not going to leave the room until Confidence comes to the party. Confidence says it is not coming to the party until Nerves leave the room.

One of them has to give in, and as the adult in the group it is up to you to take control of the warring parties.

The more that you can accept your nerves, the more your nerves are robbed of their power. Confidence is not the absence of adrenaline, so the perfect moment isn't coming. Which means the perfect moment is already here

I like to think of my nerves as an old war wound from the battle of life that's giving the old soldier gip again – which makes me smile anyway. If I can ride with an aching knee then I can ride with an aching stomach (or whatever symptom of nerves you may have.)

Confidence is NOT the absence of adrenaline. Choose your bite sizes correctly and intelligently, and do those bite sizes with or without adrenaline, with or without an aching stomach, with or without an aching knee.

If you try to ride whilst concentrating on specialist techniques focussed on conquering your nerves – breathing and counting or whatever, then it follows that your focus is NOT on riding the horse.

Focus on riding your horse, - on the perfect circle, stepping onto and off from the track at each quarter of the circle, for example

- and your nerves will necessarily – through an unavoidable cycle of distraction, experience and success - get out of your way.

"The horse wants to………"

How many times have you ridden around the arena, intending to change transition at one particular marker or fence post, only to find your mind inexplicably changed in the final millisecond?

"……..and at we'll stop at post number four. Aaaaaand whoaImeanpostnumber 5. Good boy!"

How did that happen? You had every intention of stopping / changing gait at post number four, and then your horse changed your mind for you! By means of his forward going-ness or reluctance, your horse decided to stop somewhere vaguely in the vicinity – and instead of doing the last bit of discipline to hit your mark, it was easier to change your mind.

Don't worry – it happens to us all!

You and your horse are a team…… and there are two minds in this team, and one will have more authority than the other. It is far more preferable to bring your horses mind UP into your own, and ride with 100% INTENTION. If you allow a vagueness to be included in the instruction, your horse will do more as it wishes and less as you wish – and your vagueness allows YOUR mind to be brought DOWN into the horse's!

These are matters of mind control, so be on your guard!

The end result of adopting a "that's close enough" attitude to your horse's discipline is that you risk instilling in your horse the concept that when you ask, your horse will consider your suggestion rather than obeying your order. Any parent/teacher/leader status that you possess will risk being eroded, leading to further problems down the line.

Often, after we have allowed the horse to NEARLY do as we asked, we will find excuses for the horse being undisciplined. "He wanted to / he didn't like / I can't get him to…."

How can you know what the horse wanted? He probably doesn't know himself – at least, not in the way that we humans think about it. How could you possibly know what a horse is thinking? We over-humanise horses to create a framework to justify our lack of discipline. There is NO WAY a horse was thinking like a human – and certainly no way to guess what that is. You know when you get a text from someone, and it can be read in different tones of voice to be positive or negative? If we can't even interpret a text intention, and that's from a person whose written it down clearly - what hope have you of reading your horses mind?

If you want to be a mind reader, go be a mind reader. If you want to be a rider, go ride – positively, with intention and with discipline. Be exact. Be very clear with your instructions and intentions. It is not fair to be woolly and vague, then expect the horse to know what is required of it.

(A great little help that focusses my own mind, is to imagines a film director in the arena with me, demanding very precisely the shot he wants to get and not accepting any other – and paying me handsomely to achieve it! You'll be surprised at how perfect a routine you can perform if you believe you are getting £10,000 at the end of it!)

Coming back after a break / replacing a good horse.

Let me tell you Brenda's story. Brenda had recently lost her horse Latzi after a fantastic 25 years of carefree riding. Latzi was a gentleman in every way, and Brenda was obviously heartbroken when he passed away. They do that to us, our animals.

In due course she found herself a nice new youngster, same breed and type, and began to ride again.

Brenda was surprised and somewhat amazed to find that she felt insecure, then nervous, then frightened as she continued to ride her new horse. The new horse was not a difficult chap, but just the regular youngster with regular quirks and behaviours that you'd expect – as Latzi had been when he was that age.

Brenda was shocked – and disappointed! She's been riding for years!

I wasn't surprised at all – I have heard this story SO many times.

When you think about it, Brenda, on her perfect Latzi, had not had to struggle, anticipate or out-think a misbehaving horse for 25 years! And after a 25-year break, she had jumped straight back on as if it were skills that she had used only yesterday.

Think of a skill that you last used 25 years ago. You may still be under the impression that you can do it – I promise you can't. There is a thing called skill fade – and it's real. If you are coming back into riding after 25 years – or, as in Brenda's case – coming back into riding new, unfamiliar horses after 25 years – then you simply won't be able to jump on and carry on as if you'd just been on a long tea break!

I am still firmly under the impression that I can play bass guitar – even though I sold my bass in 1991!

If you are returning to riding – or any other skill – after a break, it will pay you dividends to make a re-training plan to allow for this. The plan should begin very simply, as if you were learning for the first time. If you are easy on yourself, and patient, then not only will you re-gain your skills, but by returning to the basics and applying your conscious attention to them, you'll find that your whole experience second time around will be solidified with a wisdom and ability that will serve you always.

This methodology is why champion athletes always spend much more time re-training in the basics of their sport than any of the beginners – and is good advice for all horse riders anyway.

It is always a good idea to get back to basics.

Feel what you like but don't act on it

This little bit of advice – that's it is OK to feel how you feel – and it is not OK to act on that feeling – is one of the great things about having a discussion session at the end of every course, seminar or presentation. You just never know what great wisdom comes back to me, and I'm genuinely grateful. This little gem was from Verity, and as she worked a challenging job with children she knew a thing or two!

It goes like this :-

If you are feeling angry, that's fine. **If you hit someone because of that anger, that's not.**

If you are feeling jealous, that's fine. **If you then start breaking property because of that jealousy, that's not.**

The subject came up as we were talking about how we can sometimes feel intimidated by the people around us. If, for example, you have to go back to basics, (as one should), you may feel judged or criticised by people around you. Aha! We know this! If you feel judged or criticised by people around you, that's fine. **If you allow that to stop you getting on your horse, that's not fine.**

Because yards are yards, and people are people, you may actually be being judged or criticised. This is a most uncomfortable feeling, and you may feel shamed or embarrassed by the unkind people watching you. It's not unheard of.

But we know this one! Complete the sentence below.

If you feel shamed or embarrassed by the unkind people watching you, that's fine but if you allow ………………………………… ………… ……………………………… **, that's not!**

Relaxation techniques

I have been in two minds whether to share these two NLP techniques or not. They are *very* effective, and I have found them repeatedly useful throughout my career. So it would be remiss of me not to include them in my book of confidence with horses, as both techniques are wonderfully designed to minimise feelings of anxiety and stress.

So I wonder if you can guess my reluctance to share them?

I'll tell you the story. It was high summer, and I had just finished a Rider Confidence course, which had been super successful. It was late afternoon; the day had been beautiful and I was feeling pretty smug after a text-book hypnosis session with just the right responses from my class of clients. Sometimes you can physically see the changes in people's mindsets as they find their own transformation.

Within my courses, presentations and seminars, there is a thing called group dynamics – which is similar to peer pressure but much more subtle and subconscious. Group dynamics is a feature of human psychology that can be manipulated and teased to get people to realise how much more they are capable of. It is also the feature that is at work when, - if you are unfortunate in your choice of associates and peers - your social group allows itself to be convinced of how much LESS they are capable of – which is why individual riders and even whole groups or riders end up scared of their horses.

My handling of the group dynamics of my audience, class or clients has been developed over many years, and on this particular day it had worked like a dream. We were set to finish the day, and I had my usual discussion section to conclude the course.

The period just after hypnosis is the most powerful. Clients are relaxed and believe the day to be over, and their critical defences are down. This is the moment to pop in a few final mental images of capability, competence and confidence to send them on their way with.

One client then asked "Could I have a specific technique for when I'm stressed on the horse?"

It's a fairly relaxed moment in the day, and I may have taken a second or two longer than I should have before opening my mouth to answer. Before I could speak, however, one of the other clients helpfully piped up. "What I have found helps is to count to four on the inbreath, relax my hands and count to four on the out breath, until the anxiety drops"

Instantly the room erupted into helpful relaxation techniques to calm anxiety on a horse, all variations of the first, as each rider gave forth their accumulated wisdom.

Can you see the problem here? Whilst still in an hypnotic state, every single one of my clients was sitting there, vividly visualising *being scared on a horse and attempting to calm down!*

Remember don't think of a frog? Or the lead song from Frozen? That is exactly what was happening here, all my beautiful receptive clients happily chatting away visualising exactly how to be scared on a horse.......and I had lost control of the group. It took some fast thinking and talking on my part to bring them back round to the central issue – visualise what you DO want, not what you DON'T want.

However, dear reader, I trust you enough to not latch onto these techniques and miss the main principle of this book – to ride your horse positively / deal with your friends positively / plan out your bite sizes positively and separate yourself from the chattering masses until your subconscious falls into place.

So, on the understanding that the below is no more than 10% of your arsenal, of no more import than the parsnips on your Christmas Lunch …..here they are.

1) The Thermometer of Arousal

   When you are entering into a situation which commands your attention, you need to have the right amount of physicality, readiness and the correct, attentive state of mind to address the matter at hand. If you imagine your state of arousal to be on a scale from zero to 200, then on that scale, zero would be completely relaxed and almost asleep. Of course, completely relaxed and almost asleep is not a state in which we would need to control a horse! So we need to up our position on the scale.
   On the other end of the scale, at 200, our arousal is *so* high that we are in the realms of far too much anxiety.

   We need our state of arousal to be in the Goldilocks zone -100 - just right for the situation we are entering. I like to visualise an old-school thermometer, with the red liquid rising and falling. I take a few deep breaths, with each breath the liquid rising and falling around the 100 mark, until it settles, bang on 100, just what I need for this next situation.

   I find this quick technique takes a couple of seconds to settle anxiety/excitement/confidence levels, and away we go.

   Try it, you'll love it.

2) The Dragon Drop

This technique is useful in so many areas of life. Sit quietly in a room, and think of a situation in which you feel insecure – the issue you would like to address. Maybe it is meeting traffic, approaching jumps, riding in wide open spaces, whatever. Now, imagine installing a TV on a wall bracket anywhere in the room where you can watch your insecure issues. If you have drilled into the brickwork, please imagine vacuuming up before you leave.

Nice work. Put that to one side of your mind for a moment.

Now think of something you CAN do, confidently, competently and with no issues at all, super-confident and perfectly capable. It may be related to work, hobbies, kids, pets, dinner parties, a second language, anything - your favourite thing which you're so confident at that it barely feels like a talent. Take that super confident picture, and install THAT on a second wall mounted TV, at a different location to the first.

The locations of the TV's relative to you are important. We tend to represent positive and negative experiences by location as well as feeling, and now we have the location of the negative and insecure, and the location of the positive and confident.

In regard to our insecure, unconfident issues, just visualise the first, insecure feelings in the insecure location on the first TV. You can then look to the confident position - take the super secure feelings from the second TV and simply use your fingers to drag and drop - (which was misheard by one client as Dragon-Drop – which amused me so much that it stuck) – simply move your fingers to drag and drop the confident feelings from the confident location over to the picture of the insecure activity in the unconfident location, overlaying that insecure issue with confident sensations. You can do that again and again, feeling the confident sensation wash over your insecure opinion.

You will notice how the unconfident situation is blurred with feelings of confidence every time you do this. Do it a lot, in every situation. Get practiced.

Soon you will find that the location of the confident picture transforms into a general area of confident feelings, and the wave of your fingers (or the imagined wave of the fingers) drags those wonderful confident feelings of competency over any situation.

You can do this silently, or out loud, or in your mind, or by actually moving your fingers. Try it – it's liberating!

Conclusion

I had a really insightful conversation from a new member of staff one day as we were finishing up the yard after a busy week of three Rider Confidence seminars and two Rider Confidence Courses. We had international visitors coming in from Hong Kong and Malaysia for the following week's course, so we were discussing the reach and appeal of our service, and how to format what we do for the internet course. (www.karlgreenwood.co.uk)

As we discussed, I asked Lou "How many confident riders do you know? Actually confident and happy?"

"Oh, loads" she replied.

A thought suddenly occurred to me. "Except for professionals. I mean, amateurs, happy hackers?"

"None." Her reply was instant, un-thought about and genuine. I was shocked.

None.

I had to think. It occurred to me that professional horse riders – jockeys, filmies, stunties, carriage drivers, timber extractors, cavalry soldiers, mounted police - everyone I've ever worked with over the years – the boots on the ground as it were – are confident in their riding and horses in general.

In my own life, along with thousands of colleagues, I've ridden horses in every scenario imaginable. All sorts of horses – well trained, badly mannered, young, old.

The people who work professionally with horses are confident. Those that live the life do not constantly fret about the "What if's"

This was real food for thought. The ones doing it for a job are confident, the riders doing it for pleasure are not.

I wondered what the difference is. What do the professionals know that the amateurs don't?

Then I realised. Fundamentally, professionals do not see horses as dangerous. Unconfident hobbyists do.

I asked some pleasure riders to quote some of the words and phrases that they had heard being used to describe horses – Sharp. Wilful. Wild. Unpredictable. Big. Devious. Evil. They can smell fear. They react to your unconscious signals. Horse riding is the most dangerous activity you can do. They bite at one end, kick at the other, and are uncomfortable in the middle. You must not let a horse realise it's stronger than you.

These are all the adjectives and descriptions from people whose fundamental view of horses is that they are dangerous.

The more I observed, the more this division has become clear. If you hold the view that the fundamental property of horses is that they are dangerous, then there is a mountain of courage and determination to climb, and I take my hat off to you for the bravery you have displayed to get to this point. By bite sizes and sensible decision making, you will get there, but you have made it so much more difficult than it needs to be.

If, on the other hand, you think that horses are fundamentally safe, then the mountain disappears and you are on a flat straight and predictable road. All you need to do is walk forward. You may choose to walk in lots of little steps – that's fine. You'll get there.

Your confidence may be limited. That can be worked on. By using small and frequent, well-planned lessons it is inevitable that you will progress.

Your knowledge may be limited. That also can be worked on - reading books and taking lessons. It is *inevitable* that you will move forward.

If you choose to adopt the view that horses are fundamentally safe, and have the discipline to follow your own development plan, you will *inevitably* move forward.

This will NOT happen if you think horse are fundamentally dangerous.

This will NOT happen if you are part of a social group (your fellow riders, friends, family, internet group) that collectively believes that horses are fundamentally dangerous.

This will NOT happen if you allow yourself to feel affinity with that social groups who think horses are fundamentally dangerous.

This will NOT happen if you are afraid to incur the displeasure of those you leave behind as you progress in your riding. Your rise in status will NOT be well received – but how many of these people will help you pay the hundreds of thousands of pounds you will spend on your horses in your lifetime? That's a hundred thousand reasons why you must leave the guilt trippers and the bitching behind. Take very unkind comment as a welcome milestone on the road to success.

In order for you to move forward, it is necessary to align yourself with the riders who believe that fundamentally horses are safe, and separate yourself from the chattering masses that perpetuate and exaggerate the view that horses are dangerous.

It's time to make a choice.

This is the line that separates the two types of people. On one side is the fence leaners, the gossipers, the chatterers. The procrastinating division.

On the other side is the mounted division, including all the professionals, competitors and the professional-outlook pleasure riders. To join the mounted division will need to leave behind your insecure clucking colleagues and separate yourself.

You are going places that the chattering masses cannot accompany you. You know that horses are fundamentally safe, and it is just a simple matter of planning - and executing that plan - in bite size steps that will get you to where you want to be.

You are in the company of the capable, the knowledgeable, the professional.

You make sensible, positive decisions to succeed or learn, and distance yourself from the gossips, jokers and quitters.

You schedule the time, and find the effort, to plan - using your intelligence - and execute your bite sized steps to inevitable improvement.

Mounted Division

You ride when others sleep.
You ride when others complain.
You ride when others shun riding.
You ride when others go home.
You ride while others gossip.
You leave the crowd behind.
You are in the Mounted Division.

Look at the line that divides the professional or amateur outlook, and decide which side of it you are going to choose to place yourself.

Choose wisely.

Printed in Great Britain
by Amazon